African Science Granting Councils

Towards Sustainable Development in Africa

Teboho Moja and
Samuel Kehinde Okunade

AFRICAN
MINDS

Published in 2023 by African Minds
4 Eccleston Place, Somerset West, 7130, Cape Town, South Africa
info@africanminds.org.za
www.africanminds.org.za

The views expressed in this publication are those of the authors.
When quoting from any of the chapters, readers are requested to acknowledge all of the authors.

ISBN (paper): 978-1-928502-79-1
eBook edition: 978-1-928502-80-7
ePub edition: 978-1-928502-81-4

Copies of this book are available for free download at:
www.africanminds.org.za

ORDERS:
African Minds
Email: info@africanminds.org.za

To order printed books from outside Africa, please contact:
African Books Collective
PO Box 721, Oxford OX1 9EN, UK
Email: orders@africanbookscollective.com

Table of Contents

Acknowledgements

This book is an outcome of a project on the study of the governance structure of selected Science Granting Councils (SGCs) in Africa. The study was funded by The Carnegie Corporation of New York.

The study would not have been possible without the support and co-operation we received from the selected SGCs – Botswana, Côte d'Ivoire, Kenya and Zambia – especially under the difficult times and challenges posed by travel restrictions due to the Covid-19 pandemic.

Of immense importance, was the support that we received from the National research Foundation (NRF) South Africa from the beginning of the project to its conclusion.

The contributions made by some individuals will not go unacknowledged. They include Dr Melody Mentz-Coetzee (University of Pretoria) and Dr Dorothy Ngila.

Finally, the University of Pretoria through the Centre for the Advancement of Scholarship is deeply appreciated for believing in this project and for providing the needed support for its success.

List of Frequently Used Acronyms

KPI	Key Performance Indicators
NGO	Non-Governmental Organisation
NRF	National Research Foundation
R&D	Research and development
PPP	Public-private partnership
RSTI	Research, science, technology and innovation
SGC	Science granting council
SGCI	Science Granting Coucil Initiatie
STI	Science, technology and innovation

Knowledge Production and Policy in Africa

An Introduction

Applying knowledge generated through research to solve societal problems gained more traction following the renaissance period (14th to 17th century) and has become indispensable for some societies (Konig, 2017). Aside from the invention, innovation, and development that comes with the scientific knowledge generated through research, this knowledge is fast becoming the foundation upon which governments formulate and implement policies (Bailey, 2010; Koenig, 2005; Konig, 2017). The research–policy nexus is a topic of interest amongst scholars and governments. Many governments – for example, the United States (US) and those in the European Union – are increasingly using research products and knowledge produced to frame policy (Gluckman, 2013; Nutley et al., 2002; Soare, 2013; National Research Council, 2008).

Knowledge produced through research has the potential to influence policy decisions because it provides empirical knowledge based on studies and observable trends. These scientifically generated insights enable predictions regarding the trajectories of societal strengths, weaknesses, opportunities, and threats (Haas & Kwaak, 2017). Consequently, countries in the Global North have continuously been increasing the proportion of their gross domestic product (GDP) dedicated to funding research and development (R&D) since World War II (Harris, 2015). Governments in sub-Saharan Africa (SSA), on the other hand, have struggled to fund research at a high level and, in turn, have been reported not to rely on research evidence as a main driver of policy-making (Bailey, 2010; Naude et al., 2015). In our study, we have observed a situation that is gradually changing as governments start to draw more on research produced for policy work, but to a limited extent.

Reasons identified for the low level of funding allocated to research in Africa include poor democratic culture, over-centralisation of government functions, elite fragmentation, ideological conflicts, poor decision-making, and external influences (Bailey, 2010; Mouton, 2008; Osagie, 2012). As funds from domestic science granting councils (SGCs) have become grossly insufficient over the years, the lacuna has mostly been filled by foreign development agencies that step in to fund research agendas which are, in most cases, aligned with their own priorities (Chataway et al., 2019; Jaumont, 2016; Mouton et al., 2015; Tijssen & Kraemer-Mbula, 2018) even if relevant to those of the recipient countries.

Donor funds help but are insufficient and often difficult to access for most researchers – especially early-career researchers – due to lack of experience in operating in the highly competitive space of research-grant applications. Early-career researchers need all the support available because they form the foundation for the next generation of academics and researchers. It is such concerns that inspired the establishment of the Science Granting Council Initiative (SGCI) in Africa in 2015 with the goal of strengthening SGCs capacity for research management.

In the next section we outline the information on the SGCI in Africa and present a literature review on research arrangements in African countries – how research structures are funded and governed as well as the challenges many countries face in using knowledge produced for evidence-based policy development. We acknowledge the dearth of recent literature in this field and aim at contributing to knowledge on the topic.

Science Granting Council Initiative in Africa

The Science Granting Council Initiative (SGCI) was established to strengthen the capacities of SGCs in sub-Saharan Africa, to support research, and foster evidence-based policies that will contribute to economic and social development (Sheikheldin, 2018). Since the establishment of the SGCI, considerable developments have been tracked in member countries, although progress made individually varies by country. The initiative is funded by international donors and South Africa. Initially there were 15 members (Kenya, Rwanda, Burkina Faso, Ghana, Côte d'Ivoire, Zambia, Zimbabwe, Botswana, Mozambique, Uganda, Ethiopia, Tanzania, Senegal, Namibia, and Malawi) (SGCI, 2018, Tigabu & Khaemba, 2020; Ozor et al., 2020) but has now grown to 17 members with Sierra Leone and Cameroon as new members.[1] One of the ways through which the SGCI promotes its ideals is the Annual Forums that brings together the 17 SGCs in Africa and other stakeholders to deliberate and outline interventions on key issues affecting them (Tigabu & Khaemba, 2020; SGCI, 2018a). It is to be noted that the platform is mainly internationally funded with the South African National Research Foundation (NRF) as the only African contributor to support the platform. This has been highlighted as a problem by many state actors (Mouton et al., 2015).

Independent SGCs in the various African countries are ordinarily saddled with the task of engaging research in promoting overall development in their specific countries (Tigabu & Khaemba, 2020; Mouton et al., 2015). However, the SGCI was initiated to harness and build the capacities of these various SGCs (Ozor et al., 2020; Tigabu & Khaemba, 2020; Mouton et al., 2015). According to Ozor et al. (2020), the roles of the SCGs in sub-Saharan Africa are to manage research, design and monitor research programmes based on the use of robust science, technology and innovation indicators, support knowledge exchange with the private sector, and to establish partnerships between councils and other science system actors.

The idea behind the initiative is to harness the potentials of research in furthering evidence-based policies, promoting science, technology

---

1   https://sgciafrica.org/about-us/

3

and innovations and generally enhancing socio-economic development on the continent (SGCI, 2017, 2018a, 2018b). As Cloete et al. (2018) state, the SGCI in sub-Saharan Africa is a reflection of the international community's commitment to supporting Africa's research potential for more coordinated scientific growth. While the agenda for Africa's development is well articulated in Agenda 2063[2] and the implementation strategy provided through Science Technology and Innovation Strategy for Africa 2024 (STISA) – especially on science, technology, innovation and policy – the practical collaboration needed to deliver remains an issue (Tigabu & Khaemba, 2020; Hanlin et al., 2020; SGCI, 2018a; Sheikheldin, 2018). According to Tigabu and Khaemba (2020), the reluctance of governments to set up SGCs that are independent and can receive funds from the donor community in their countries is due to a lack of trust and suspicion of the interests and agendas of international donors.

The lack of scholarly literature on the impact and contributions of the SGCs in supporting and funding research that can contribute to the socio-economic development of member countries in the African continent (Tigabu & Khaemba, 2020; Hanlin et al., 2020) may be a factor responsible for governments' lack of information and their reluctance to set up SGCs in their various countries. The fact that many international donors and organisations are willing and have been facilitating and funding various research in various countries have made them drivers of national STI objectives (Tigabu & Khaemba, 2020; Mouton et al., 2015). This may also be a contributory factor to the negligent attitudes of many African countries to set up government agencies such as SGCs.

It is important to note that while the SGCs in Africa reflect the overall goals and interests of many countries on the African continent, their modus operandi does not necessarily align with national approaches (Mouton et al., 2015). Equally, there is the question of divergent interests between donors and governments. As Tigabu and Khaemba (2020) state, there is a tension between the state (politics) and SGCs over research priorities and areas of jurisdiction. The situation seems to be changing as indicated in our own study (Moja & Okunade, 2022) which found that

---

2   Aspiration 1: A Prosperous Africa, based on Inclusive Growth and Sustainable Development.

there is in fact a greater level of alignment of priorities in the countries studied.

Though the SGCI was not established to promote the increase in funding for individual SGCs, it has been criticised for its inability to promote and influence a comprehensive and stable funding arrangement for SGCs in the various countries (Tigabu & Khaemba, 2020; Mouton et al., 2015).

There are notable achievements in some member countries, whilst others have not been so laudable (Tigabu & Khaemba, 2020; Mouton et al., 2015). For instance, the SGCI (2018a) noted that due to the efforts of the SGCI, there was the initiation of a national development plan in Uganda, Namibia, Mozambique and Rwanda while on the other hand nations like Burkina Faso, Senegal and Cameroon were yet to deploy similar efforts to enhance the development and consideration of STI in their national development initiatives. Compounding the affairs of the SGCs and SGCI is the question of coordination within science systems amongst others (Oyelaran-Oyeyinka et al., 2018; Mouton et al., 2015). As have been noted, many nations within Africa have existing local science, technology and innovation platforms and initiatives mostly within government departments responsible for incorporating science technology into national development (Tigabu & Khaemba, 2020; Ozor et al., 2020; Bailey, 2015). In most cases, these arrangements are not well structured, coordinated or funded for the tasks they were set up for (Mouton et al., 2015).

The establishment of the SGCI in Africa as an overarching platform is a positive move to address the problem of coordination and structure which are lacking in many SGCs, especially in francophone countries (Fosci & Loffreda, 2019). Researchers have observed that there is also a proliferation of research funding councils aligned with sectoral and political interests which makes synergy and collaboration efforts difficult, especially in identifying priorities within the same countries and regions (Chataway et al., 2019; Bailey, 2015). Where SGCs do not exist, research funding arrangements are made within government departments and ministries with overlapping duties relating to disbursement of funds for science and technology research (Mouton et al., 2015). With such structures, research projects outside the scope of government aims and objectives are not likely to be funded which limits the reach and exploratory value of scientific research (Oyelaran-Oyeyinka et al., 2018). This has been argued to reflect the political and historical leanings and trajectories of these countries which either prioritise or undervalue the role of science and technology for national development (Mouton et al., 2015).

Addressing Africa's socio-political, socio-economic and security challenges not only require adequate focus on developing its science technology and policy infrastructures but doing so independently to enhance growth which is generally lacking in many countries. Therefore, the question of establishing independent SGCs funded by government remains a concern (Hanlin et al., 2020; Tigabu & Khaemba, 2020) as well as how independent they are. According to Oyelaran-Oyeyinka et al. (2018), the lop-sidedness of the governance structures of national councils not only affects the successful development of science councils but also the participation of private sector in science technology and innovation projects. The vital role of the private sector in driving science technology and evidence-based policies has been repeatedly reported in several studies and reports (Tigabu & Khaemba, 2020; Ozor et al., 2020; SGCI, 2018a; Khaemba, 2018a, 2018b, 2018c). This role is hindered by the lop-sidedness that tends to characterise national councils especially in cases where the interests of state differ considerably from private organisations. This, however, does not eliminate the importance both actors play in the institutionalisation and development of a science and technology driven economy.

According to the 2019 SGCI survey carried out on the 15 SGC member countries, there was generally weak capacity within SGCs for communication and effective engagement with the private sector (SGCI, 2019). Empirical findings discussed in subsequent chapters confirm this as a major shortcoming which SGCs need to address. While many SGCs had good interactions and relations with government institutions and departments for political aims, the structures did not allow for effective communication and engagement with the private sector especially in partnership and inclusion for implementation of science and technology (Fosci & Loffreda, 2019; Chataway et al., 2019; Mouton et al., 2015). Bailey (2015) relates a finding in her study of eight research councils and commissions across Africa, that

All were led by a governing body comprising a council/board or commissioners, headed by a chairperson – except for the Mozambique M-CNAQ, which was governed by a president, not a national state president, and nonexecutive directors. The chairpersons and members were appointed either by the state president/prime minister or by the minister responsible for Tertiary Education/Higher Education (TE/HE). The number of council members or commissioners varied from 9 to 25. The day-to-day work of councils/commissions was undertaken by secretariats of salaried staff and headed by a chief executive officer who was appointed by the council or commissioners, the minister or the state president. (Bailey, 2015, 180).

This structure according to scholars undermines the independent status of these councils and commissions which are needed to protect against political interference and ensure the advisory functions of the commissions both to the private and public sectors (Bailey, 2015; Cloete, Bunting, et al., 2015; Cloete, Maassen, et al., 2015).

These issues indicate some of the salient and institutional setbacks that science and research granting councils and commissions have had to navigate in the course of enhancing evidence-based policies and science and technology in the African continent (Tigabu & Khaemba, 2020; Koehn & Uitto, 2015; Mouton et al., 2015). Moreover, the failure of many African governments to implement the stipulated percentage of national budget according to the Lagos Plan of Action continues to reflect the poor inclination of African governments to academic and research development (SGCI, 2017, 2018a).

Although SGCs supposedly indicate the commitment of the various nations to the development of science and technology in their various countries, the overwhelming evidence from the few available studies of these commissions/councils tend to indicate otherwise (Tigabu & Khaemba, 2020; Mouton et al., 2015). It seems more to be the case that these councils are set up for political reasons rather than for national and regional development. The inherent structural and governance issues identified in the countries with existing SGCs reveal that as much as governments are interested in investing in research, science and technology, they are only willing to invest in these endeavours to the extent that it benefits an existing government politically (Arvanitis & Mouton, 2019; Fosci & Laffreda, 2019; Cloete & Maassen, 2015).

It is in this context that salient issues that border on the objectivity, vision and broad engagements of the existing SGCs are not taken seriously. The fact that major decisions by these SCGs are made by government-appointed chairpersons and other stakeholders (Bailey, 2015) are indicators that objective ideals and initiatives with little bearing on existing political agendas may not receive requisite support for implementation. While there is need for a clear-cut definition of the vision and functions of SGCs in Africa apart from their political partners that tend to interrupt their activities (Tigabu & Khaemba, 2020; Chataway et al., 2019), governments in Africa may need to show more dedication to the development of science and technology as well as evidence-based policies by providing necessary funds (Arvanitis & Mouton, 2019; Cloete, Maassen, et al., 2015; Musiige & Maassen, 2015). The commitment to education as Fosci and Loffreda (2019) and Cloete et al. (2018) observe is still very much below expectation in light of the AU's vision of becoming a major economic hub by 2063. Achieving this necessitates that African governments commit to supporting SGCs in Africa (Chataway et al., 2019) by making funds available for research.

Of particular importance is the use of empirically-based research, especially in relation to science, education, security and governance on the continent. This is important for harnessing the rich intellectual resource of the continent as well as discouraging the brain-drain syndrome facing the continent currently (Fosci & Loffreda, 2019; Cloete, Maassen, et al., 2015). The non-use of research by the government has been a recurrent reason for the stalemate between government and academic actors on the continent (Fosci & Loffreda, 2019; Van Schalkwyk, 2015; Bailey, 2010) due to misconceptions and misperceptions on the role of research for development (Bunting et al., 2015; Musiige & Maassen, 2015).

Objective of the study

While there is limited literature on the research–policy nexus in sub-Saharan Africa and the utilisation of research outcomes (Bailey, 2010; Broadbent, 2012), other studies have shown the disconnect between research and policy on the African continent (Mouton, 2006, 2008;

Naude et al., 2015; Olomola, 2007). No literature could be identified that focused on the internal dynamics of relationships within and between SGC officials and other relevant bodies, and how these dynamics could influence the level of funding allocated to the agency that distributes funds to researchers. Understanding the interactions of key stakeholders in the research allocation and distribution is what framed the study. In particular, the interest was in understanding the governance structures and relationship dynamics within and between the management staff of SGCs and other relevant bodies such as members of boards. More specifically, the study sought to understand the strategies, challenges, and opportunities associated with these structures and relationships, with the ultimate goal of understanding and exploring strategies for increasing research funding levels and promoting the reliance on research for development in Africa.

Methodology

This study adopted a qualitative approach using a phenomenological case study method. A phenomenological approach explores an issue based on the everyday knowledge and perceptions of specific respondent subgroups (Lindgren & Kehoe, 1981). Qualitative research is unique in that it enables the collection of culturally specific information about the values, opinions, behaviours, and social context of a particular population. Therefore, what distinguishes the qualitative research method from other research methods is the opportunity to do an in-depth study and analysis by obtaining first-hand information from respondents.

Primary data was collected qualitatively using key informant interviews. Informants interviewed were selected purposively from amongst SGC staff and governing board members in four African countries – namely, Botswana and Zambia in Southern Africa, Côte d'Ivoire in West Africa, and Kenya in East Africa. These countries were selected to represent the three SGCI regions and include a mixed sample of both independent SGCs and one located within a government department. South Africa is included in some instances as a benchmark, especially for a comparative analysis. Table 1 shows the SGCs that formed part of this study and the number of the participants from each that were interviewed.

TABLE 1 Science granting councils in the four case-study countries and interviewees from each

NAME OF COUNCIL	COUNTRY	STATUS	YEAR ESTABLISHED	NO. OF INTERVIEWEES
The Department of Research, Science and Technology (DRST)	Botswana	Non-independent	2004	4
Strategic Support for Scientific Research Programme (PASRES)	Côte d'Ivoire	Independent	2007	4
The National Research Fund (NRF)	Kenya	Independent	2013	1
The National Science and Technology Council (NSTC)	Zambia	Independent	1997	1

Data collection faced various challenges due to the Covid-19 pandemic. The first challenge was establishing contact with the original six SGCs selected for the study. Since we could not achieve that, we decided to work with the four that we got responses from. The second challenge related to identifying sufficient number of officials and policy-makers to interview, as they were facing internal challenges trying to cope with the pandemic. The main contacts in each country made several attempts to set up appointments for us with the policy-makers and board members, but their efforts did not yield the number of participants we had hoped for. Furthermore, the researchers could not travel to the selected countries to interact with the SGC officials and observe modes of operation. However, as an alternative, online interviews were scheduled with them via Zoom. Where necessary, follow-up questions were sent via email. It was late in the study that limited travel became possible to verify some of the data that was collected during the lock-down period.

The sample of key informants interviewed included eight principal officers and two policy-makers.

Limitations of the study

The study was designed with the goal of talking to more policy-makers and members of the SGC governing boards than were ultimately recruited to participate. We had anticipated that it would be challenging to talk to policy-makers; however, due to disruptions related to the Covid-19 pandemic, the challenges were significantly exacerbated. Appointments were repeatedly cancelled as officials sought to address more pressing issues. We had also hoped to interview more members of the SGC staff and members of their boards, but executive management working closely with them struggled to secure appointments for us – especially via Zoom. Appointments would have been easy to secure if we were in the country. It is our belief that had we been able to visit the countries physically, the interview process would have been easier. This was confirmed by one member of the executive management who guaranteed us access if we were to visit in person. However, travel restrictions prevented us from making any in-person visits to the case study countries.

The Politics of Research, Knowledge Production and Policy in Perspective

Research as a tool for public policy

There is a relationship that exists between agencies of government and researchers when it comes to research engagement for policy purposes. St John (2013) explicitly examined the power play that exists between both parties in the process. In other words, he x-rayed the dilemma academics face when contracted to conduct policy research. Rawls (1971, 2001) explaining the relationship between researchers and policy-makers using social contract theory, noted that both parties share institutional interest in advancing public good through fairness for citizens. However, current political realities reveal that the opposite is usually the norm. The roles of policy-makers and policy researchers are distinct. While policy-makers are responsible for promoting politically worthwhile agendas, policy researchers promote "education science through theoretical frames and evidence" (St John 2013, 4).

St John (2013, 122) insists that "the aim of research should not be to promote agendas but to provide information". Sen (2009, 180) also notes that "a person's voice may count either because her interests are involved or because her reasoning and judgement can enlighten a discussion".

Therefore, researchers must draw a fine line between the agenda of the policy research funders and the evidence of the research. This is usually a Herculean task for researchers who work with private research firms as they are caught betwixt and between.

According to St John (2013) government-funded projects are contracted to private research firms by government agencies. Researchers working with such firms are tasked with a basic responsibility which is to ensure that they get work done in a way that the firm does not lose its contracts. This implies that the outcome of the research should reflect the expectations of the funding agency *ab initio*. This distorts the research process.

St John (2013) further noted another class of researchers. These are researchers based in policy centers in the university who equally engage in research for state agencies with an interest in specific research agendas. This class of researcher enjoys some level of autonomy in carrying out their research. And they enter into such research because it is both their area of expertise and in the common interest of both parties. With this kind of relationship, the process could be jointly decided upon or otherwise. Nevertheless, the outcome of the research is not influenced by the funding agencies in any way.

St John identified with Habermas' concept of public reasoning to public policy. As qualified by Macey (2000), Habermas distinguished between strategic or goal-oriented action and communicative action which seeks to build understanding. Habermas also differentiated between open strategic action that discusses goals and closed strategic action which is based solely on authority (Habermas, 1987). In other words, Habermas sees strategic action as an action targeted at setting goals and achieving such while communicative action is concerned with answering the "why' question regarding problem existence, and both parties identifying and evaluating strategies for addressing such inequalities and injustices (St John, 2013).

There are four contexts of policy research based on Habermas's frames of discourse (Habermas, 1987). These frames of discourse can be adopted in examining the roles that the government and researchers play in policy research. In other words, the frames can be utilised to explain the dynamics of power at play between government agencies and researchers in the use of scientific research in government policy.

Equally, it should be noted that the analysis of the four frames of action below provides an understanding of what each entails and, as such, prepares researchers to identify, navigate and perform effectively under any context.

TABLE 2: Explaining the government and researcher roles in policy research using Habermas' Frames of Discourse

FRAME OF ACTION	GOVERNMENT ROLES	RESEARCHER ROLES
Instrumental Frame	The government agency desires evaluative studies to inform policy decisions	Researcher produces evaluative research desired by the government
Closed-Strategic Frame	Government agency seeks studies that support its policy initiatives	Researcher changes methods to fit agency demands with findings subject to government approval
Open-Strategic Frame	Government agency seeks new ways to tackle current policy challenges	Researcher focuses on issues concerned with new ideas. Potential for collaboration on interpretation of the research.
Communicative Frame	Government agency work with researchers to find new ways to solve challenges.	Researchers collaborate with policy-makers using qualitative and quantitative methods to address inequalities

Source: Compiled by the author/ adapted from St John (2013).

The above four modes of interaction take place between policy-makers and researchers involved in policy studies under different circumstances. According to Table 2, the instrumental frame is the context where the government simply desires to evaluate its policies. They develop the programmes and the research that follows is used for assessment and programme evaluation. This scenario gives the researcher the freedom to carry out research and evaluate government policies with minimal interference. St John (2013) identifies this as the norm in the United States, especially in the 1960s and 1970s as provisioned by the Elementary and Secondary Education Act and Higher Education Act. The government is in a position to choose to use the research products to justify their work, or to ignore the results.

In the closed-strategic frame, government acts in a manner to obtain research that is in support of their policy initiatives. Here, the researcher's results have to be favourable and are subject to the approval of the government agency commissioning the policy study. American President Reagan used this frame in the revision of federal programmes in the 1980s. In contrast, the open-strategic frame involves the government agency seeking new insights into policy challenges. Thus, the researcher is encouraged to provide new approaches to current problems.

Finally, the communicative frame refers to situations where the government works together with researchers to create innovative solutions. Researchers collaborate with various stakeholders to conduct their research. According to Gluckman (2013), some European projects have adopted this approach by seeking a diversity of opinions for policy action.

SGCs are institutions representing the government and as such could either enjoy total or partial autonomy depending on the legislation that established them. This affects and sometimes dictates the kind of research to be funded by the SGC. However, researchers in higher education institutions have the choice to respond to calls for research funding and have autonomy in terms of the research they will pursue, and therefore have the freedom to conduct research that does not necessarily promote government agendas but can neverteless provide information that can be used for policy (St John, 2013, 122). It is only in circumstances where research is commissioned that the research carried out supports specific research agendas. It is this context that needs to be taken into consideration to address the frustrations expressed by policy-makers that research does not necessarily address their development agendas.

A policy dialogue amongst key stakeholders could be one way of resolving the issues raised by policy-makers in order to clarify the role and ways that research contributes to development. It is therefore suggested that various modes of the Habermas's Frames of Discourse can be adapted to clarify roles, and research can benefit society in various ways.

While it is imperative for the utilisation of research outcome for policy formulation, it is equally important for the research community to fashion ways in which knowledge produced is relatable and usable. This is discussed in the following section.

Knowledge transfer and implementation

Research institutions have increasingly become concerned about their relevance in society and in particular about meeting the needs of their immediate and wider society through knowledge production and transfer. An increasing trend in the field globally is the push for the private sector and governments to use cutting-edge research for the broader societal benefit (Tumuti et al., 2013). Universities are continuously seeking strategies to become more engaged in society and to have impact that contributes to development. Ssebuwufu et al. (2012) underscores the triple mandate of university teaching, research, and outreach (or community service) as a mandate to contribute to development. Ferreira and Carayannis (2019, 353) refer to the latter as the "third mission" of the university and argue that it should be considered to be the most important manadate of the university. Whereas universities have often been fixated with teaching and research, the outreach arm of the mandate is increasingly being called upon to bridge gaps between the universities and the wider society and directly involve universities in developmental efforts (Tumuti et al., 2013; Adelowo et al., 2017). In the USA the knowledge transfer from universities to industries has been buttressed by the 1980 Bayh-Dole Act that enabled research institutions to patent and license their knowledge for societal benefit.

The present discourse on university–industry linkages is framed by the triple helix which serves as a heuristic tool that facilitates an understanding of the interaction between three actors (Awuor, 2013) – universities, industry, and government – that need to work together to transform knowledge into development. Jacobs et al. (2019) note that the triple helix indicates the importance of the university and shows that it needs to work in consonance with the other two actors to diffuse knowledge into society. The university therefore has to work on changing the public perception that it is an "ivory tower" that stands aloof and detached from the society (Tumuti et al., 2013). Empirical findings from the study buttresses the preceding as it was discovered that the three actors play an important role in knowledge production and would equally need to partner for such produced knowledge to be converted for the good of the citizenry.

Ideally, university–industry linkages form an essential part of collaborative partnerships which creates opportunities for developing activities and programmes such as research (joint) and development (R&D); job and internship placements for students and young graduates; representation on governing/advisory boards; research centres; staff exchanges; and innovation/commercialisation initiatives. In addition, these partnerships could also facilitate the effects of STI on the economy through "increased skills transfer and development; absorption of skilled talent into the labour force; and STI advancements and transfer" (National Research Foundation, 2019, 2–3).

The preceding shows the imperativeness of the university–industry linkages as it enhances development through knowledge transfer that the partnership offers. However, knowledge transfer for societal benefit is being called into question in the African continent. With the continent lagging in development indices, there is now a clamour to directly involve science and technology into the innovation required to drive development. The African Union has set the pace in this regard. The African Union Science Technology and Innovation Strategy for Africa (STISA) of 2014 sets out a 10-year plan for the continent to mainstream science and technology into plans for Africa to reach the Sustainable Development Goals of 2030 (Chataway et al., 2019). The African Union's endorsement of the importance of university–industry linkages sets the agenda for African countries to work with as they strive towards the attainment of their goals (Oyelaran et al., 2018). As a result, four years later, almost two-thirds of African countries had created science technology and innovation policies (Oyeleran et al., 2018).

University–industry linkages have continued to grow in importance. However, the focus of most of this knowledge transfer is often in the field of science and technology. This is because of the supposed relevance of those fields to the innovation of products and services by firms and companies (Fillippetti & Saravona, 2017). This unfortunately puts other fields such as humanities and social sciences at a disadvantage due to the perceived lack of clear-cut translation into tangible economic products. However, as noted in the preceding chapter, the contrary has been discovered as a research study carried out in Senegal by *Consortium Pour La Recherche Economique Et Sociale* (CRES) on anti-smoking regulation prompted new policy actions that solved an age-old problem in the nation that had hitherto received scarce attention by the policy-makers even when it was of no less national value (Diyamett et al., 2019). Jacobs et al. (2019) noted that South African universities emphasise science fields to the detriment of other fields in university–industry linkages. The drive of universities to work with industries has led to the emphasis on the prospects of profit-making for the research institutions rather than direct societal benefit. Ssebuwufu et al. (2012) in their study of university–industry linkages in 133 African universities noted that there was a tendency to focus on commercialisable knowledge rather than socially beneficial ones. They further warn African universities to refrain from crossing ethical lines when carrying out research in partnerships with industries.

There are a number of ways in which universities can strengthen their linkages with industries. Fillippetti and Saravona (2017) suggest more employment of researchers with business and industrial employment history. The universities could take advantage of the network of contacts of the new employee to foster lasting relationships with the industry. In addition, Ssebuwufu et al. (2012) advocate for the training of academic staff in entrepreneurship. This would equip faculty with entrepreneurial skills that would be helpful in their engagement with the business world and also guide their research to make it more commercialisable.

The above is equally important as the South Africa NRF Industry Partnership Strategy (2019) noted that critical skills production is a vital strategic focus of the national innovation system in South Africa. Academic–industry programmes play an important role in fast tracking academic career pathways for emerging researchers such as doctoral students, junior scholars and postdoctoral fellows, and in producing a highly skilled workforce that is capable of transferring intellectual and technical expertise to industry. This can be achieved if academic staff are well equipped with the needed entrepreneurial skills.

Skills transfer, as noted, is another benefit for universities and industry. Tumuti and Thoruwa (2013) discuss the partnership between Kenyatta University and Equity Bank. This linkage was borne out of the desire of the two stakeholders to work together for the benefit of the local communities in Kenya. The Directorate of Community Outreach and Extension established a five-year partnership with the bank to train 3,000 students to participate in community development services across the country (Tumuti et al., 2013). This partnership empowered the students to receive specialised training and gain valuable work experience in their communities. Jacobs et al. (2019) observe the participation of South African universities in three societal interventions – the Living Labs, Rural Innovation Assessment Toolbox, and Community University Partnership Projects. The Living Labs enabled the local communities to get involved directly in knowledge production with research institutions so as to create useful community-centred knowledge and policies.

The difference between South African Living Labs and those implemented in Western countries is the active involvement of the rural communities. The Rural Innovation Assessment Toolbox involved provision of local communities with innovative options to drive development while the Community University Partnership Projects saw community leaders and researchers come together to share knowledge on resolution of joint challenges. Jauhiainen and Hooli's (2017) study on indigenous knowledge use in innovation systems in Namibia also notes that Living Labs bring community members together and sparks their interest in contributing to solutions of everyday challenges that plague their communities. Ssebuwufu et al. (2012) from his study of 133 universities across Africa opines that universities are taking steps to promote the societal benefit of their research but face challenges including inadequate funding and poor support from African governments.

Chataway et al. (2019) highlight various ways that four African countries in East Africa are embedding knowledge transfer in their developments. Rwanda has created specific recruitment policies for students into science technology, engineering and mathematics (STEM) fields while Tanzania has weaved research funding around specific research needs. The Ethiopian government mapped out relevant development areas and began a funding campaign accordingly while Kenya ensured the societal benefit of research was tailored towards the objectives of respective political administrations.

Despite the increased involvement/effort of the government, it has been found to be insufficient and politicised with low levels of funding (Ssebuwufu et al. 2012; Adelowo et al., 2017; Chataway et al., 2019). Jauhiainen and Hooli (2017) argue for the important place of indigenous knowledge of the community in creating development in Namibia. They note that universities should incorporate local communities who are guardians of indigenous knowledge in the overall knowledge production needed to revamp the Namibian economy. Awuor (2013) identifies the achievements of the African Knowledge Transfer Partnership in Kenya to include creation of new products, new sources of raw materials, better technological techniques as well as development of high-quality graduates from universities.

SGCs are the major bodies tasked with the responsibility for ensuring the engagement of research institutions in development, particularly on the African continent. The SGCs set the criteria for funding research and help disseminate the findings of studies by the academic community (Oyeleran et al., 2018). Chataway et al.'s (2019) study of SGCs shows that they face the dilemma of either upholding the traditional system of academic excellence or the contemporary focus on societal beneficial research. The traditional system is alternatively perceived to adopt the "Republic of Science" approach that considers the research community to be free of external pressures and permitted to pursue academic excellence without recourse to its impact on development (Ssebuwufu et al., 2012). This approach considers the pure academic merit of research work such as publication in peer-reviewed top international journals. This could prevent researchers from making vital contributions to the society (Adelowo et al., 2017).

Meanwhile the embedded autonomy approach sees research as subject to the needs of the society. The drive to fit into the developmental focus of African governments could alienate the science councils from the African research community who may look for international funding to continue the "Republic of Science" approach and implement foreign agendas (Chataway et al., 2019). Badat and Prozesky (1994) also maintain that the clash between the "Republic of Science" and embedded autonomy approaches pose a dilemma for the science granting councils. The solution could be to reduce the level of "Republic of Science" approach of the science governing councils and make them more democratic thereby focusing on the developmental needs of African countries (Badat & Prozesky, 1994).

Research-based policy through a global lens

The use of research in formulating policy gained traction after World War II and became a standard of best practice for governmental and non-governmental organisations towards the end of the 20th century (Bailey, 2010). Consequently, nations of the Global North are striving to base their policies on empirical research. There are several examples of this globally. A study carried out by Haas and Kwaak (2017) demonstrated that, in the Netherlands, research plays a major role in policy decisions. There is robust use of evidence, as Gluckman (2013) has demonstrated, in New Zealand in the framing and implementation of policies. In the United Kingdom (UK), there is a Centre for Evidence-Based Policy and Practice, which is funded by the Economic and Social Research Council. Its task is to improve the accessibility, quality, and usefulness of research; develop methods for appraising and summarising research relevant to policy and practice; and advise those in policy-making roles through its dissemination function (Nutley et al., 2002). In India, the National Institute for Educational Planning and Administration, an academic institution, was set up by the Ministry of Education to provide policy advice based on their research.

The UK government is estimated to invest over GBP 3 billion annually in research and requires funding applicants to demonstrate the contribution of their research to society and the economy (Harris, 2015). In the US, government policy relies heavily on research outcomes. For example, the US National Research Council (NRC, 2008) reported the following with regards to the important role research plays in the policies of the US Department of Housing and Urban Development (HUD). According to the NRC,

> research on major housing issues and programs tends to be ongoing, with new research projects being developed on the basis of findings of earlier research and on program outcomes. Each HUD administration is able to draw on that body of research, each is able to add to it during its term, and each leaves behind it a body of completed studies and studies in process that are intended to be of use to its successor. (NRC, 2008, 150)

The Global North has demonstrated that research has a significant role to play in the development of any society. However, in our search we did not find literature on the specific use of academic research outputs for policy formulation in the Global South. The following section explores the extent to which research evidence is utilised for policy formulation and development purposes in various countries in Africa.

Research-based policy: regional reflection

This study chose not to draw from the literature on the Global South as a whole but instead focused on case studies from Africa. The literature reveals that there is limited work on the relationship between knowledge production and development in Africa (Bailey, 2010). Available studies indicate that there has been an enduring disconnect between research and policy. Not only is most research generated in seeming isolation, but there is also a lack of institutional support and enabling frameworks for knowledge to be transformed into policies and initiatives that contribute to societal advancement.

For instance, although government is a major funder of research in South Africa – especially in the public sciences (Mouton, 2006) – a study by Naude et al. (2015) revealed that research is not the main driver of policy in South Africa; rather, current contextual realities, costs, logistics, and people (clinicians, funders, and NGOs) are the primary influencers of policy. The study further found that research evidence is sometimes perceived as unavailable, inaccessible, ill-timed, or not applicable (Naude et al., 2015). A similar study conducted by Olomola (2007) in Nigeria demonstrated that, even with the existence of policy-oriented research organisations in Nigeria, policy decisions do not draw from relevant research.

Olomola (2007, 165) argues that there are 'major pitfalls in the research–policy nexus, including gaps in policy initiation, poor culture of policy development, policy confusion and uncertainties, and inadequate linkage mechanisms. He further notes that, in Nigeria, the research and policy communities seem to work at cross-purposes. Mouton (2008) acknowledges the resilience of African researchers when he notes that there is still ongoing and vibrant research in countries where there is little government support for research, poor institutional facilities, and various other challenges. The central question thus becomes: Why is research evidence often ignored by policy-makers in Africa?

In contrast, a few studies have found positive examples of the research–policy nexus functioning effectively in Africa. For instance, an empirical study conducted on institutional policies implemented across four African states (Ghana, Uganda, Zambia, and Sierra Leone) demonstrated a 'relatively high' use of evidence in policy debates, especially in Zambia (Broadbent, 2012, 2). The study also shows that there is a system in place in Kenya that ensures that research outcomes are valorised.

Having established that research evidence is generally not integral to policy formulation in Africa, it is imperative to explore the factors underlying this reality. The next section outlines hindrances to research driving policy formulation in Africa.

Challenges associated with research-based policy

In Africa, the factors hindering widespread adoption of research-based policy formulation are complex, spanning from the political structures to governance and challenges associated with nation-building. Bailey (2010) identified specific challenges affecting the research–policy nexus in Africa – namely, pseudo democracy (which is antithetical to pragmatic and popular decisions), over-centralised polity, constant antagonism with civil society groups, elitist but popular decision-making, and ideological divisions which engender biases and frictions amongst decision-making and research stakeholders.

Another commonly cited problem is that policy-makers come into contact with enormous amounts of information daily but have very little time to read, absorb, and assimilate relevant information. Some politicians or decision-makers are ignorant about the availability of policy-relevant research, or, when they are aware, can be "dismissive, unresponsive or incapable of using research" (Bailey, 2010, 20). There is also the problem of the politicisation of evidence, which leads to research outcomes either not being utilised or being used in a way that support political agendas (St John, 2013).

A recent study by Lugo-Gil et al. (2019) identifies several challenges related to utilising research for policy. The first challenge is that researchers' questions, timelines, and objectives do not always align with those of decision-makers. The second is that very few researchers and decision-makers work to establish mutually beneficial relationships. Third, research conducted in academia often fails to address the questions that programme and policy decision-makers want answered. The fourth challenge is that most research findings are presented in a manner that is not accessible to non-experts, and the products created do not meet the information needs of decision-makers. Finally, they noted that linking research to decision-making can be resource-intensive, and some government agencies possess limited capacity to do this.

As indicated earlier, St John (2013) identifies four frames of action that are used to examine the roles of the government and the researcher in the research-policy nexus for government-initiated research that could be helpful in understanding the relationship between research and policy (see Table 2). A common feature of all four frames of action is the influence that the government has in the process, particularly in cases where they are the initiator of the research. The nature and degree of influence varies, however, it determines the extent to which government dictates the research approach. Under the instrumental and closed-strategic frames, the level of influence of the government is high and they play a large role in determining the direction and goals of the research. Under the open-strategic and communicative frames, government influence is lower and collaboration higher, making these the preferred frames of action for supporting an effective research–policy nexus. It is equally important to note that the government has influence because they provide funding for such research. International donors and grant providers are also significant sources of funding for research in Africa. Nonetheless, insufficient accessible funding continues to pose a major challenge for research in Africa. The next section explains the importance of funding, identifies the major funders, and reveals the role of African governments in this regard.

Challenges in research funding in Africa

Research is dependent on funding from various actors such as government, foundations and donors, industry, and the private sector. The importance of science, technology and innovation (STI) to the economic growth of the African continent has been asserted by various high-profile agencies and reports, and governments are displaying a growing interest in funding STI research across the continent (Mouton at al., 2015). The journey to knowledge-based economies for Africa began with the 1980 Lagos Plan of Action, expected to be fully implemented by 2000, where an agreement was reached that 1% of the national annual budget of all African states would be dedicated to Science and Research (SGCI, 2017). Furthermore, in line with African Union Development Agency–NEPAD objectives (AUDA–NEPAD, 2017), many African governments have again committed themselves to increasing their GDP dedicated to R&D since they could not meet the deadline set by the 1980 Lagos Plan of Action.

The implementation of these agreements has been slow and inconsistent; in some cases, implementation is non-existent. A study by Mouton et al. (2014) found that the 1% target set for Africa remains elusive, with average expenditure on R&D in African countries being in the range of 0.3%–0.4%. In the four countries sampled for this study, the average expenditure ranges from 0.08%–0.8%. However, our findings revealed that these figures are increasing, as governments are showing more commitment to funding research in Africa.

The research funding gap in African states has been filled to some extent by foreign bodies, governments, and jointly owned organisations such as the African Capacity Building Foundation, the African Economic Research Consortium, the Global Development Network, and the Secretariat for Institutional Support for Economic Research in Africa (Bailey, 2010). While such partnerships are welcome, the funding priorities and strategic goals should ideally be negotiated so that the relationship is mutually beneficial to all partners.

Scholars have debated the driving forces and politics behind partnerships between such grant making organisations and research institutions in Africa. According to Jaumont (2016), who studied the efforts of specific US-led foundations aimed at strengthening higher-education capacity in sub-Saharan Africa, underscores the complexity and nuances in the grantor/grantee relationship in the definition of priorities. While the relationship between a partner who needs resources and the one who has the resources to give is often inherently unequal in terms of power and influence, Jaumont (2016) cautions against overly simplistic and extreme stances, and describes the positive outcomes of these partnerships as follows:

American foundations have helped shift the national priorities of African countries toward the field of higher education by convincing international funders and national governments that higher education is the key to economic development. This has resulted in larger investments from all stakeholders and a shift toward modernisation, institutionalisation, and internationalisation in African universities. (Jaumont, 2016, 88)

As STI is gaining national and continental attention (Chataway et al., 2019; SGCI, 2017, 2021), it is anticipated that more research funding will be made available by governments. This interest has been strengthened by the fact that the developmental initiatives of many African countries depend on the science and technology sector to provide effective solutions to developmental challenges in the form of renewable energy, medical innovations, and eco-friendly power sources (Tigabu & Khaemba, 2020). Evidence of this shift in focus to STI can be seen in increased funding and the establishing of platforms for such endeavours through SGCs (Khaemba, 2018a; Tigabu & Khaemba, 2020). Several African nations have set up SGCs, with the aim of promoting scientific research to address developmental issues. The next chapter presents the four countries that were the subject of study so as to understand the broader context, the establishment of their SGC, its functions, and the arrangements in relation to research activities. For the one country without an SGC, the context and how research functions are supported and funded are presented including the broader landscape of research in the country. References are made to the National Research Foundation based in South Africa as a reference point adopted for the study.

Case Studies of Countries in Africa

Higher Education Systems and Science Granting Councils

Four case studies were identified for this study. They are Botswana, Côte d'Ivoire, Kenya and Zambia. South Africa was included as a reference point. To present the case studies, we first outline the higher education system in each country, exploring its research arrangements. We focus on the national higher education systems because of the role that higher education plays in producing research for the nation. A survey of the higher education landscape in the countries in the study reveals a rather disparate system of education. Chataway et al. (2019) however notes that a common factor among higher education systems in African countries is the theoretical commitment of government and public sector to improving education but less observable momentum in practice.

Botswana

Higher education system in Botswana
Botswana's higher education landscape has undergone considerable transformation and change from its humble beginnings. Following the 7-5-4 education system, higher education is preceded by seven years of

primary-school education and five years of secondary-school education (Mbiganyi, 2018; Damane & Molutsi, 2015; Molutsi, 2009). According to Molutsi (2009), the basic education landscape in the country after independence was significantly improved by the government through continual investment in education resulting in 81% literacy rate among its population in 2003. Botswana has also been recognised as one of the developing nations to maintain international standards in commitment to education with over 25% of its annual budget allocated to education (Molutsi, 2009). From having no tertiary education institution in 1966, there are currently over 40 tertiary institutions in Botswana comprising 10 universities, 30 vocational and technical training centres, 4 teacher training colleges, and 2 colleges of education (Botswana Hub, 2022; Molutsi, 2009). The previously jointly owned University of Botswana, Lesotho and Swaziland located in Lesotho was the first tertiary institution that catered for prospective students from Botswana on a quota system basis that admitted a total of 5,000 students from the three countries (Baliyan & Moorad, 2018; Mbiganyi, 2018; Molutsi, 2009). The curriculum was essentially focused on producing administrators and teachers to enhance the country's educational sector. These statistics have shaped access, affordability and utilisation of higher education in the partner countries.

The University of Botswana was established in 1982 following the breakaway of Lesotho from the higher education arrangement they all had (Mbiganyi, 2018; Molutsi, 2009). The focus at the former university on humanities, social sciences and education rather than on science, technology and innovations, had far reaching effects on the nation's development necessitating a review of the higher education curricula (Adekanmbi Kasozi, Seabelo & Batisani, 2021; Molutsi, 2009). Also, this bias led to the reliance on foreigners and expatriates for science and technology development in the country, and also the sponsorship of young Batswana to study in foreign countries to enhance local human resource development (Molutsi, 2009). These strategies were expensive mitigation strategies; hence the drive to establish local institutions and diversify the higher education curricula to include these vital areas. Higher education covers a vast area of specialised occupations, technical and vocational needs for the country such as agriculture, wildlife game wardens, nursing, paramedics, police, prison wardens, artisans and technicians etc. (Molutsi, 2009). These specialised areas are provided with a diploma certificate after a period of training while tertiary education institutions such as universities and specialised institutes and colleges take a minimum of four years for undergraduate studies and also offers graduate and doctoral studies (Tladi & Nleya, 2017; Molutsi, 2009).

Higher education in Botswana is currently supervised by the Ministry of Tertiary Education, Research, Science and Technology (MTERST) to accommodate the various higher education institutions while the Tertiary Education Council established in 1999 but operational in 2003 oversees the quality of higher education in the country (Molutsi, 2009).

The Ministry facilitates the development of research, science and technology in higher education through its various departments and parastatals that provide specific educational needs for both institutions and students (Republic of Botswana, 2022).

Funding for higher education in the country comes essentially from the government for public institutions while private institutions are generally funded by tuition fees and donor support (MTERST, 2021; HRDC, 2021; Baliyan & Moorad, 2018). The University of Botswana, Botswana International University of Science and Technology, the Botswana University of Agriculture and Natural Resources, and Botho University are some of country's best and public institutions while the Limkokwing University of Creative Technology and the Ba Isago University are some of the private universities in the country (Republic of Botswana, 2022; Botswana Hub, 2022).

Student enrolment in these institutions have continued to witness considerable increase due to increasing demography, government sponsorship of education and establishment of public and private tertiary institutions in the country (Human Resource Development Council, 2017; Tladi & Nleya, 2017; Molutsi, 2009). According to Adekanmbi et al. (2021), higher education enrolments reached nearly 60,000 pre-Covid. Molutsi (2009) observes that the enrolment gap between public and private tertiary institutions is gradually closing, even though there are cumulatively more public institutions due to issues of quality and standards, massification and preference for university education rather than vocational education. A key factor facilitating the enrolment in private tertiary education is the availability of government sponsorship and loans for students in the country to pursue specific courses (HRDC, 2021; HRDC, 2017). The creation of the Botswana Innovation Hub (HUB) amongst other initiatives by the government is one of the strategies engaged by the government to further the actualisation of a literate citizenry with a globally competitive human resource base.

The overall higher education landscape in Botswana reveals an ambitious government with clear aims and objectives for actualising its goals for national development (Damane & Molutsi, 2015; Molutsi, 2009). While the government is on a set path by committing significantly to tertiary education, the need for funding and technology development to expand educational opportunities to rural regions in the country is evident (Adekanmbi et al., 2021). Also, the roles of international organisations and NGOs in funding research prospects and tertiary education in Botswana have been recognised in areas such as health, education, environment, and agriculture (UNDP, 2021; De Beers Group, 2021).

With an allocation of BWP 407 million (equivalent to USD 36 million), the government of Botswana remains the highest facilitator of higher education in the country, even though challenges of massification, infrastructure, and use of ICT in learning persist (Adekanmbi et al., 2021; The Botswana Gazette, 2021; MTERST, 2021).

Botswana has been making efforts to promote research in the country. The government, along with various universities and research institutions, supports research initiatives across different fields. Key areas of research in Botswana include public health, natural resource management, wildlife conservation, sustainable tourism, climate change, and social sciences. The Botswana Institute for Technology Research and Innovation (BITRI), Botswana Institute for Development Policy Analysis (BIDPA), University of Botswana, and Botswana University of Agriculture and Natural Resources (BUAN) are among the key research institutions in the country.

Current data is challenging to access. With the current growth in the higher education sector and research initiatives supported by several sectors, the University of Botswana's productivity and scholarly research publications in 2010 stood at 1,002 with no patents (University of Botswana, 2010). The data show modest and consistent growth in the number of publications from 2005 to 2010 (Tabulawa & Youngman, 2017). In another study, an average of 275 articles were produced per annum between 2009 to 2016 by the national research system in Botswana (Cloete et al., 2018). It is to be noted that Botswana is a relatively small country with a population of 2,359,609 million in 2022 (Statistics Botswana, 2022).

Science, technology and research in Botswana

As shown in the preceding section, countries in the Global North that use research to inform development tend to establish various research councils and centres. Botswana seems to address the challenges of the drought, health, and the non-diversification of the country's economy, through development plans poised towards science technology and innovative research (Weaver et al., 2005). This was evident in the various national development plans and policies that targeted the improvement of the country's socio-economic and human capital development as well as the healthcare sector (Weaver et al., 2005). The National Research, Science and Technology Plan identifies the specific priorities for investment and action for Botswana's national development plans (Samboma, 2019; Weaver et al., 2005). This Plan outlines the socio-economic issues and challenges facing the country and the specific actions to be taken by government to address these issues in the various national development plans and for investors (Nkwe, 2012; Weaver et al., 2005). This system of planning and projection has helped to put the country on a path of development as the specific actions required for each sector of the country's economy are outlined. For instance, in the NDP 9 and NDP 10, the Plan outlines the specific actions of government as:

- committing to a research expenditure of 1% of gross domestic product which is the minimum level for emerging innovative economies;
- allocation of research funding on a competitive basis for the purpose of engaging more relevant and efficient research focused on priority development areas for the country;
- the establishment of the Botswana Research, Science and Technology Funding Agency to manage the competitive funding;
- the establishment of a task team to merge the National Food Research and Technology Centre and the Department of Agricultural Research into a National Food and Agricultural Research Centre;
- the merging of the Botswana Technology Centre and Rural Industries Promotions Company (Botswana) to form a new institution;
- the incorporation of the NDP's objectives into all institutional plans of government-funded research entities to ensure full alignment with national system of innovation;

- development of performance indicators for all research agencies to monitor the implementation and impacts (actual and intended) of government-funded research; and
- the training of highly specialised post-graduate researchers who will be required to lead the research within the identified priority areas by Universities and Centres of Excellence in the country. (Weaver et al., 2005, viii)

Commitment to the above areas and objectives is indicated partly by the setting up of the science funding commissions/councils in the country as well as partnership with other countries both within and beyond the sub-region (Khaemba, 2018a; AAS, 2017; Mouton et al., 2014).

Botswana's journey to the establishment of a science council began with the process for establishing the Research Science Technology Innovation policy which brought together several public and private organisations to revise the science and technology policy of 1998 (Mbiganyi et al., 2015). This revision was in response to the rapid technological evolution, National Development Goals/Plans, Vision 2016 and the Millennium Development Goals (Mbiganyi et al., 2015). While the government through the Ministry of Finance is the major funding agency for developmental research and science technology innovation, the country has also embarked on partnerships with regional and international public and private organisations to enhance its investment in science research (Khaemba, 2018a; AAS, 2017; Mbiganyi et al., 2015; Teng-Zeng, 2009). According to the Botswana National Research, Science and Technology (2005) report cited in Mbiganyi et al. (2015), the country had invested 0.43% of its GDP in STI which is below its own stipulated 1% (Weaver et al., 2005) and also below the recommendation by the South African Development Community and the African Union of which Botswana is a member (Mbiganyi et al., 2015).

Coordination of research, science, technology and innovation in Botswana
On the structure of the financing of research, science, technology and innovation (RSTI) in Botswana, findings indicate that there are challenges that have been identified in comparison with several other SGCs in sub-Saharan Africa (Mouton et al., 2015; Bailey, 2015; Mouton et al., 2014). First, the coordination and funding of the RSTI lies strategically within the government and its policies, and funding for projects are

structured in line with the goals and objectives of government (Tigabu & Khaemba, 2020; Chataway et al., 2019; Bailey, 2015). While this may not be entirely negative, as Mbiganyi et al. (2015) observes, it has the tendency of slowing down the innovative pace of science research especially when it has to do with areas or subjects beyond the scope of government's development goals.

According to Figure 1, the operationalisation and implementation of the RSTI policy lies within the Ministry of Infrastructure, Science and Technology (MIST) which is made up of four departments: Department of Research Science and Technology (DRST); Department of Radiation Inspectorate; Department of Building and Engineering Services (DBES); and the Department of Corporate Services (Mbiganyi et al., 2015). Some parastatals within the MIST with similar mandate of implementing the RSTI policy are the Botswana Institute of Technology, Research and Innovation (BITRI) and the Botswana Innovation Hub (BIH) (Mbiganyi et al., 2015). The DRST under the MIST was also mandated to work with the Ministry of Communications, Science and Technology; Ministry of Agriculture; Ministry of Education and Skills Development; and the Ministry of Health to provide leadership in science and technology through the provision of an enabling policy and legislation environment and coordination of science and technology activities in the country (Mbiganyi et al., 2015). The Ministry of Finance, however, provides the major bulk of funds needed for these projects and programmes making the DRST and other departments and parastatals dependent on government for financing (Mbiganyi et al., 2015).

As a result of this dependence, investment in the implementation of the RSTI was reportedly low. There is a failure to translate knowledge, education and learning into activities that promote STI as well as low conversion of research outputs to products, systems and services with socio-economic benefits (Mbiganyi et al., 2015).

While the DRST has the priority of focusing on networking and collaboration, technology, research and innovation capacity, human resources, institutional capacity and knowledge base (Mbiganyi et al., 2015), the implementation and attainment of these strategies have been rather slower than intended, various partnerships notwithstanding. The lack of commensurate partnership with the private sector has been identified as a factor affecting the attainment of stated objectives by the DRST (Khaemba, 2018a). Although most of the financing comes

FIGURE 1: Coordination of RSTI in Botswana

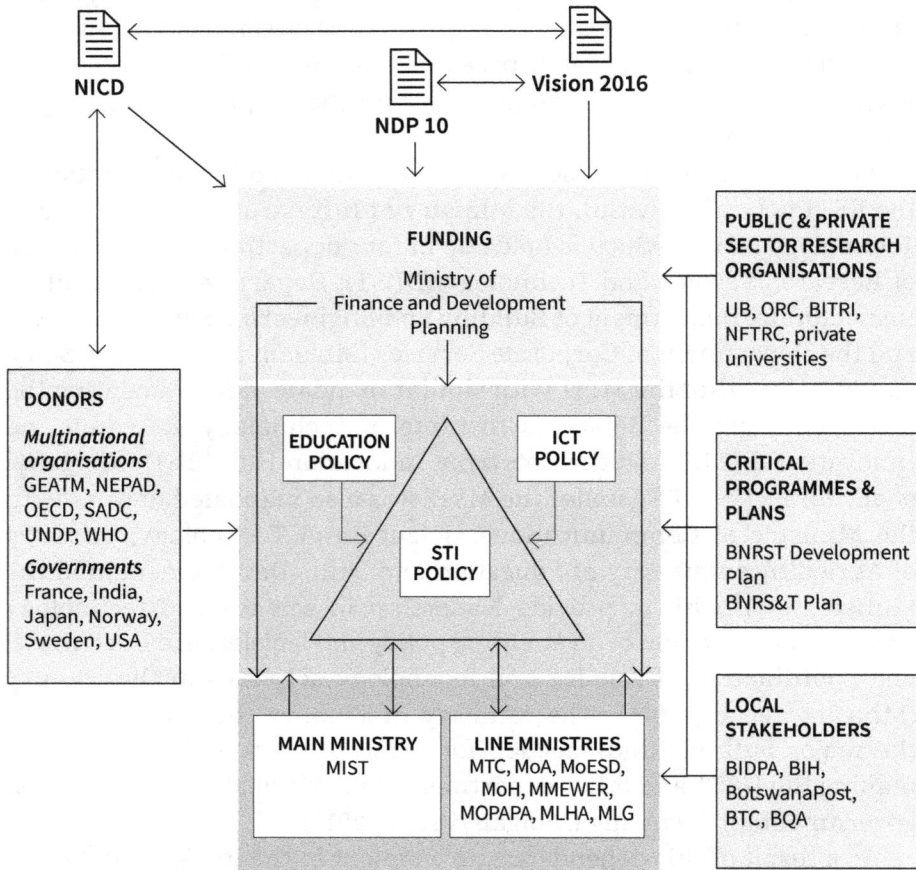

from the government, scholars have noted the need for public–private partnerships (PPPs) to enhance the availability of advice for necessary innovations as the private sector more often than not determines the trend and trajectory of the market economy (Khaemba, 2018a; Mbiganyi et al., 2015). Effective partnership with the private sector will ensure that necessary support for government's innovation and technology goals will be made readily available and will also provide the necessary information and trajectory needed to enhance government's position (Tigabu & Khaemba, 2020; Mbiganyi et al., 2015; Mouton et al., 2014). This is important considering that the major research activities in the country are funded and coordinated by the government, thus leaving little opportunity for what could be perceived as interference from the private sector (Chataway et al., 2019; Khaemba, 2018c; Bailey, 2015; Mbiganyi et al., 2015). This according to Tigabu and Khaemba (2020) has been a challenge for SGCs in sub-Saharan Africa since governments are willing to use these councils and commissions for their national goals rather than organisations for necessary consultation and support in national development.

Other challenges that have been identified in the implementation and coordination of the RSTI policy in the country is the lack of funding in the various sectors that are necessary for attaining the stated objectives in research science and technology innovations such as energy and internet connectivity (Khaemba, 2018a; Mbiganyi et al., 2015). Studies indicate that although there has been considerable investment by the Botswana government in the ICT and energy sectors, this is not reflected in the consumer population thus threatening the viability and possibility of achieving its various national goals (Samboma, 2019; Mbiganyi et al., 2015). Furthermore, the need for a coherent national policy to drive the RSTI policy has been underscored by scholars (Khaemba, 2018c; Mbiganyi et al., 2015) as the existing DRST does not have the necessary autonomy to act as an independent SGC. The various bodies and organisations notwithstanding, the autonomy and coordination required to drive independent research especially in innovations are still lacking (Tigabu & Khaemba, 2020; Chataway et al., 2019; Khaemba, 2018a). Although the National Research Development and Innovation Coordinating Council is proposed as the SGC to coordinate research and STI in the country, there is yet to be the formal establishment of this body (Khaemba, 2018a).

Relating the weakness and failures of the existing state of STI implementation in the country, Khaemba relates that "low innovative capability, low research collaborations and failure to utilise indigenous knowledge ... threats include overreliance on state funding for STI, low participation by private sector and lack of proper monitoring and evaluation" (Khaemba, 2018a, 11). Even though the country outlined some achievements in scientific publications combined with a good investment climate and well-established communication infrastructure in a self-administered SWOT analysis, the fact remains that the funding and coordination arrangements in the country pose more of a threat than an enabler to the attainment of its national objectives (Khaemba, 2018a). While public investment and participation in the development of the research science and technology is important for the country, the total dependence and coordination of the operations and financing of STI by the government does not allow for the necessary flexibility required to drive innovative research. For one, the fact that much of the research findings are not used by the government (Khaemba, 2018a; Mbiganyi et al., 2015) seems to explain that government attention is mostly focused on achieving political and economic gains rather than receiving actual results.

Also, the lack of an independent unit driving the monitoring and evaluation process of government-related activities in research reduces the credibility of the various STI policies and frameworks sponsored by the government (Khaemba, 2018a; Mbiganyi et al., 2015; Teng-Zeng, 2009; Weaver et al., 2005).

While the necessary partnership with regional and international entities are vital for enhancing its technical and technological capacity for pursuing and achieving its goals (Isaacs et al., 2021; Khaemba, 2018a; AAS, 2017), the establishment of an independent body to coordinate STI activities and programmes is more advantageous (Mouton et al., 2014; Bailey, 2015). Private institutions and organisations, for example, may find it easier to relate with such organisations than with government parastatals and organisations which essentially represent and serve the interests of government (Khaemba, 2018a; Mbiganyi et al., 2015; Nkwe, 2012). Furthermore, partnerships will be more effective when the private sector is poised towards implementing and influencing government to implement necessary developmental initiatives (Isaacs et al., 2021; Nkwe, 2012).

Overall, research, science and technology innovation in Botswana is more likely to breed healthy competition and innovative ideals when STI bodies and organisations are structured to interact more objectively with the private sector as well as with other SGCs in Africa. This is also likely to attract more funding opportunities for the development of STI in the country.

Côte d'Ivoire

Higher education system in Côte d'Ivoire
The education system in Côte d'Ivoire is largely structured after the French system and divided into basic and higher education sub-systems (World Bank, 2019b, 2021; Universalia, 2018; Oyeniran, 2017). Basic education (pre-primary to lower-secondary school) covers the compulsory education of children aged 3 to 16 years while higher education comprises the education of students 17 years and above from the uppper-secondary to tertiary institutions (World Bank, 2019b; Oyeniran, 2018; Oyeniran, 2017). The higher education system includes vocational training and diploma certification (World Bank, 2021; Oyeniran, 2018).

Higher education institutions are broadly divided into public and private institutions within the country: there are 6 universities and over 20 specialised tertiary institutions under the supervision of the Ministry of Higher education and Scientific Research (MESRS) and over 180 private and faith-based higher institutions (CIRES, 2016; World Bank, 2021). While the overwhelming numbers of higher education institutions in the country are privately owned, records indicate that the public institutions are more poised towards science research and innovation than the private institutions (CIRES, 2016). According to the CIRES assessment of the academic institutions in the country, the private institutions are more geared to training and education of their students than the public institutions which are more focused on scientific research (CIRES, 2016). Research subjects and departments are recorded in the foremost public university than in other universities in the country and these are mostly carried out by students and senior research staff (Dosso et al., 2020; CIRES, 2016).

Some of the prominent public higher education institutions in the country are the University of Abidjan-Cocody (founded 1958), Felix Houphouet-Boigny University, University of Bouake, Nangui Abrogoua University, and the University of Korhogo (World Bank, 2021). These universities and the several other tertiary institutions receive funding for development research primarily from government but also private sources such as international donors, private firms, funding organisations, etc. (World Bank, 2019b, 2021; Universalia, 2018). Private institutions are essentially funded by tuition fees and donations.

This system also makes room for considerable scientific research which the nation's education policy observes to be very vital to attaining national development goals. As such, while the Ministry of National Education and Technical Vocational Education and Training (MENETFP) oversees education at the basic level, the MESRS oversees education at the higher level by providing necessary technical, financial and managerial support needed to steer higher education in the direction of national development (World Bank, 2019b, 2021; Universalia, 2018).

A World Bank (2021) report noted that besides these two overarching bodies, there were 12 other sectoral higher education institutions to address specific areas in the education system of the country. The National Council for Higher Education (CNESER) oversees the quality of higher education in the country by accrediting and evaluating higher education institutions (World Bank, 2019b, 2021). The Ministry of Higher Education and Scientific Research (MESRS) has 10 directorates that further address specific education- and research-related issues in the higher education system amongst which are the General Directorate for Standardisation and Quality, General Directorate of Higher Education and Research Information Systems Management, Directorate of Higher Education and Professional Integration, Directorate of Scientific Research and Innovation, a Directorate for Higher Education amongst others (World Bank, 2021). Funding for research and innovation in higher institutions within the country falls under the purview of the General Directorate of Scientific Research and Innovation (GDSRI) and this body since its establishment has committed over CFA 500 million to the research and innovation in higher institutions (Universalia, 2018).

Higher education in Côte d'Ivoire according to reports has recorded appreciable results considering the country is recovering from a recent civil war (World Bank, 2021; Oyeniran, 2017, 2018). According to the World Bank (2021), there has been a consistent increase in higher education enrolment since 2005 with an annual average growth rate of 2.5%. Higher education follows the License-Master-Doctorate (LMD) system in a 3-2-3 year scheme after the French education system (World Bank, 2021).

The World Bank (2021) report while noting the country's progression towards national development also observes the relatively low level of scientific research from the various universities and tertiary institutions. According to the report, while considerable opportunities for funding is provided by donors and public institutions, the country produces fewer than 400 scientific articles in international journals each year. This report, however, observes several institutional and structural challenges in the country's public institutions that contribute to hinder the optimal functioning of these institutions. Some of these are increased demographic pressures on available infrastructure, quality control challenges, overburdening of public sector in funding higher education in the country, lack of ICT infrastructure, lack of proper harnessing of the higher education system across public and private institutions, and recurrent strike actions by staff and students (World Bank, 2019b, 2021). As such, while basic education in the country allows for relative technical and vocational empowerment, higher education in the country continues to grapple with infrastructural and technical issues prevalent across the African region. Generally, however, the higher education system in Côte d'Ivoire tends to be more pragmatic than other countries within the region.

Côte d'Ivoire has steadily been growing its research and academic community. The country has several universities and research institutions actively engaged in scientific research across various fields. Key areas of research in Côte d'Ivoire include agriculture, health, environmental conservation, biodiversity, social sciences, and economics. Some of the prominent research institutions in Côte d'Ivoire include the *Centre National de Recherche Agronomique* (CNRA), *Institut Pasteur de Côte d'Ivoire*, *Institut de Recherche pour le Développement* (IRD), and Université Félix Houphouët-Boigny. These institutions conduct research, promote scientific collaborations, and contribute to the development of the research ecosystem in the country.

Based on the available data, Côte d'Ivoire was recorded to have between 2 and 10 PubMed publications per annum for the period 1996–2005, which rose to more than 1,000 articles cumulatively between 2000 and 2014 (Saric, 2018). We could not find data for subsequent years to assess any increase in publications.

Science, technology and research councils in Côte d'Ivoire
The focus on institutionalising and enhancing a science, technology and research council in Côte d'Ivoire was restored with the new National Development Plan (PND) 2012–2015 instituted by the government of President Alassane Ouattara (IMF, 2016; CIRES, 2016). The PND 2012–2015

enhanced the commitment to science and technology for economic growth, through the Strategic Support for Scientific Research Programme (PASRES) established in 2007, which is the foremost body tasked with organising science, technology and research in Côte d'Ivoire (Dosso et al., 2020; Adjei & Nintin, 2018; Forson, 2017; Van Lill & Gaillard, 2014).

Founded in 2007, the body was the result of a joint cooperation between Switzerland and Côte d'Ivoire. The body receives funds to enhance economic and social development in the country (Van Lill & Gaillard, 2014). The activities of PASRES include funding research aimed at reducing poverty, allocating grants for training young researchers, providing support to research facilities to enhance access to scientific information, provide support for the establishment of a national science funding centre in the country, and enhance exchange programmes between the north and south (Adjei & Nintin, 2018; Van Lill & Gaillard, 2014). Between 2007 when it was founded and 2014, which was the latest data we could find, PASRES has funded over 200 researchers in the country (Van Lill & Gaillard, 2014). However, before the establishment of the PASRES, several councils and ministries had been established to enhance the growth of scientific research in the country even though performance has been below expectations (Dosso et al., 2020; Forson, 2017; Van Lill & Gaillard, 2014).

In 1971, the Ministry of Scientific Research was created to coordinate the mainly cultural research centres and councils which had been created and managed by the French prior to independence (Van Lill & Gaillard, 2014). This ministry has been closely associated with the economic success of the 1970s as research opportunities and interests grew during this period with the result that more researchers were trained, and research centres were established and equipped (Van Lill & Gaillard, 2014). However, in 1981, exactly a decade after the establishment of the ministry, the deficiency of science research in higher institutions was evident. This was remedied by restructuring the Ministry of Scientific Research into the Ministry of Higher Education and Scientific Research (Van Lill & Gaillard, 2014). This was an attempt to incorporate higher education students and staff into the growing research body in the country. The economic strides and progress made within this period in the country necessitated further developments in the country's tertiary education and science research sector so that between 1981 and 1993 the ministry coordinating research and higher education underwent several changes in an attempt to capture emerging realities in the implementation of scientific research in the country (Van Lill & Gaillard, 2014).

These developments were such that by 1993, the ministry was renamed the Ministry of Higher Education and Technological Innovation; and in 1998 it was split into Ministry of Higher Education and Scientific Research, and the National Center for Agronomic Research (CNRA) to address the main areas of research interest in the nation (Van Lill & Gaillard, 2014). However, due to the political upheavals that characterised the nation in the 1990s and early 2000s, the functionality of these ministries, especially in relation to funding research for development, greatly waned due to adverse economic growth (Adjei & Nintin, 2018; Forson, 2017; Van Lill & Gaillard, 2014). Hence by 2003, the Inter-Professional Fund for Agricultural Research and Council (FIRCA) was established to further manage agricultural research institutions in the country. Still greatly hindered by the effects of the civil war within this period, the PASRES was founded with mainly international support from Switzerland as part of external efforts to build lasting peace and enhance economic growth in the country (Van Lill & Gaillard, 2014).

The Ivorian Center for Economic and Social Research (CIRES) is the national body tasked with coordinating Côte d'Ivoire's research environment and capacities in the social sciences (CIRES, 2016). The aim of the body is to coordinate and recommend strategic developmental reforms for both qualitative and quantitative growth of the nation (CIRES, 2016). The center also facilitates research by granting funds to researchers as well as build research capacity in the country. The CIRES through the 'Doing Research in Social Science' (DRSS) Index has established six dimensions for covering research for national development in the nation (CIRES, 2016). These six dimensions are also the national index for measuring the success of scientific research development in the country and cover the following areas: the availability and quality of physical infrastructure and human capital; capacity building activities and incentives; documentary resources; information and communication technologies, and networking (CIRES, 2016).

Due to the long years of civil unrest in the country, the major centres of science output for the nation are a few research institutions. Hence, researchers are mostly the students and staff of the emerging universities (public and private) and research institutions in the country (CIRES, 2016).

As part of renewed efforts to enhance scientific research and growth in the country, the Ministry of Higher Education and Scientific Research in August 2012 issued the *Document Supporting the Implementation of Research Programmes in Côte d'Ivoire* (Van Lill & Gaillard, 2014). The aim of the policy, amongst others, was to encourage partnership between private and public research and training institutions for enhanced innovative projects (Van Lill & Gaillard, 2014). The document recommended in accordance with the Lagos Plan of Action, that 1% of the country's gross domestic product (GDP) be committed to financing research in Côte d'Ivoire (Van Lill & Gaillard, 2014). This was agreed to by representatives from the government, research councils and educational institutions across the country although Kouadio (2012 in Van Lill & Gaillard) observed that the financial commitment to research in the country was still less than 0.5%. However, the IMF (2016) report indicates that marked improvements have been made as a result of the implementation of the PND in relation to access to primary and secondary education especially with the building of new schools and employment of staff (IMF, 2016). For tertiary education and research councils however, the funding required for conducting science, social and economic research are mostly inadequate with several processes of scrutiny before approval.

Coordination of research, science, technology and innovation in Côte d'Ivoire
The evidence from the SGCs in Côte d'Ivoire as in other SGCs across sub-Saharan Africa indicates that the coordination of research activities is mostly under the control of the government (Dosso et al., 2020; Iizuka et al., 2018; Adjei & Nintin, 2018; Forson, 2017; Van Lill & Gaillard, 2014). Even in cases of international partnerships, the results indicate that government plays a much larger role than the private sector in funding research (Adjei & Nintin, 2018; Forson, 2017; Van Lill & Gaillard, 2014). While this may not all together be negative, the political inclinations and unstable political terrain of the nation remain common threats to the actualisation of a truly independent research sector. Although calls for synergy between the private and public sector have been made by the government (Van Lill & Gaillard, 2014), the fact that the majority of the funding opportunities for research come from the government, and the coordination of the major research councils are drawn from existing government structures, tend to undermine the independent status

required for SGCs to function optimally (Adjei & Nintin, 2018; Iizuka et al., 2018; Forson, 2017; CIRES, 2016). For example, the PASRES, which is the apex body for funding research in Côte d'Ivoire, is administered by a decision-making body, an advisory body and an implementing agency (Van Lill & Gaillard, 2014; Forson, 2017).

The Minister of Scientific Research, the representative of State Secretariat for Education and Research of the Swiss Confederation (SER) and the Director of the leading house decide on the allocation and release of funding for scientific research (Van Lill & Gaillard, 2014). The Steering committee or decision-making body of the organisation consists of six members, drawn from the Swiss councils in Côte d'Ivoire, the Ivorian government, the science council in Côte d'Ivoire and NGOs (Van Lill & Gaillard, 2014). While the scientific council has 11 members drawn from universities and research centres across the nation, their duties are merely advisory (Van Lill & Gaillard, 2014). This puts the overwhelming force of decision-making and allocation of funds on the government of Switzerland and Côte d'Ivoire, and invariably means that projects that do not reflect national or foreign policies do not gain the necessary attention and support required. This trend is also observed by Forson (2017) who noted that "although Ivory Coast does not have an elaborate STI policy plan, funding for the activities of the Directorate General of Scientific Research and Technological Innovation (DGSRTI) and its technical directorate for research and innovation is provided by the National Agricultural Investment Program established in 2010" (Forson, 2017, 10).

He further observed that while the country has made considerable strides in its scientific research developments in comparison with its West African neighbours, there remains much to be achieved in terms of coordinating research in the nation (Dosso et al., 2020; Forson, 2017). The major challenge associated with the excessively central mode of coordinating SCGs in Côte d'Ivoire as in other sub-Saharan African countries is the limitation of funds (Dosso et al., 2020; Adjei & Nintin, 2018; Forson, 2017). As research findings have repeatedly shown (Dosso et al., 2020; Forson, 2017), government funding for STI in Africa remains below policy recommendations and global standards. Hence by being the major funding mechanism for scientific research, research councils and institutions have to struggle for adequate resources and empowerment to implement the innovation aspect of STI (Dosso et al.,

2020; Adjei & Nintin, 2018; Iizuka et al., 2018; Forson, 2017). One of the main hindrances resulting from this limitation of research funding is the lack of enthusiasm to fund innovative research. As Dosso et al. (2020) state, the innovative part of STI is not usually reflected in the funding initiatives of African governments especially in Côte d'Ivoire chiefly because the country is recovering from its political crisis. As such, since the government is the major coordinating and financing body, only research projects that reflect government policies, aims and political orientation receive considerable attention for funding (Dosso et al., 2020; Adjei & Nintin, 2018; Forson, 2017).

This is one of the reasons highlighted for the gross lack of researchers in the country as well as in the West African sub-region (Dosso et al., 2020; Forson, 2017; CIRES, 2016; Van Lill & Gaillard, 2014). Côte d'Ivoire had a total of 3,832 researchers and academic staff in 2014 which was approximately 17 researchers per 100,000 inhabitants instead of the prescribed 90 researchers per million inhabitants and 193 per million for lower-middle income countries (Dosso et al., 2020; CIRES, 2016). Closely associated with the foregoing is the problem of partnerships with the private sector. The overarching role of the government and international organisations in STI research in the country has resulted in a lack of morale for adopting STI policies and innovation by the private sector (Adjei & Nintin, 2018; Forson, 2017; Van Lill & Gaillard, 2014). Although Adjei and Nintin (2018) note that there is dearth of national laws and legislation to foster such cooperation between private institutions and international governments and funding agencies, they also observed that there is considerable low interest in research findings by the private sector. This may not be totally disconnected with the fact that the coordination of science technology and innovation research lies substantially with the government which is more politically oriented (Dosso et al., 2020; Adjei & Nintin, 2018; Iizuka et al., 2018; Forson, 2017).

Also, the fact that transnational institutions have little contact with the private sector in terms of funding research, is also a challenge to the coordination and execution of research in the country (Adjei & Nintin, 2018). The limitation of government's coordination of the country's STI and research endeavours is evident in the skill mismatch of graduates as well as the lack of competence of graduates to meet labour demands (Adjei & Nintin, 2018). These can however be addressed when there is adequate partnership and collaboration between the private and public sectors as well as between the domestic and international research councils in the country (Dosso et al., 2020; Adjei & Nintin, 2018; Iizuka et al., 2018; Forson, 2017). Although political fragility is a definite factor in international collaborations and partnerships, attention must be turned towards incorporating the private sector as well as empowering them to engage more actively in scientific research and innovation (Adjei & Nintin, 2018). While the government focuses on raising socio-economic structures and attaining economic feats, there is the need to promote innovative research by not only implementing policies and recommendations that increase financial commitment, but also incorporate the private sector into the coordination and management process of disbursing these funds (Dosso et al., 2020; Adjei & Nintin, 2018; Forson, 2017). Furthermore, having appreciated that role of scientific research and innovation in enhancing national development, there is need to improve diversified research especially in the areas of innovation for the rich agricultural sector of the nation. More importantly, there is need to diversify funding agencies in the country to enhance research.

Kenya

Higher education system in Kenya
The higher education system in Kenya is structured after the British system with the nation's oldest tertiary institution, the University of Nairobi, sharing links with the University of East Africa and the University of London prior to 1970 (Mukhwana et al., 2020; Koyi et al., 2020; Odhiambo, 2018; McCowan, 2018; Mulongo, 2013). The current higher education landscape of the country is a rapid departure from what it used to be from the 1970s through to the 1990s where only two universities constituted the higher education system: the University of Nairobi and Moi University, the latter founded in 1984 (Koyi et al., 2020). Kenya has 74 accredited tertiary institutions, founded and accredited between 1990 and 2017 to boost the higher education sector to meet national goals (Cloete et al., 2018). These institutions comprise universities, technical institutions, teacher training colleges and agricultural institutions all under the supervision of the Ministry of Education, Science and Technology (World Bank, 2019a). The Ministry is responsible for the formulation of educational policies, and the coordination and supervision of tertiary education across the country (Mkhwana et al., 2020; McCowan, 2018).

47

The country's Commission for University Education (CUE) is tasked with the responsibility of regulating and ensuring quality assurance and standards through the accreditation and licensing of universities and colleges, and of curricula (Koyi et al., 2020; World Bank, 2019a). Higher education in Kenya is the final four-year component (under the 8-4-4 system) for specialised study and further options for advanced postgradaute studies (master's and doctorate degrees) (Ndemwa & Otani, 2020).

Higher Education in the country is recognised by Koyi et al. (2020) as a catalyst for the production of elite workforce and socio-economic activities, especially in the production of human capital resources for national development. As a result of the nation's investment in higher education and learning, five of its national universities have been named among the top 100 universities in Africa.

Several of Kenya's higher education institutions have also made considerable contributions to science and technology in the African region. For example, the University of Nairobi designed effective low-cost locally sourced medical equipment to improve maternal, infant and child health (Maobe & Liping, 2020). Moi University initiated a Waste for Wealth project that entailed the use of organic waste to make tables to curb plastic waste and create a new source of income. Odinga University of Science and Technology initiated the use of clay coolers to preserve fruit and vegetables and prevent post-harvest losses (World Bank, 2019a). All of these strides were engendered through adequate funding and support of higher education in the country.

Although Kenya's higher education landscape shows considerable government support for science-based innovations and research, Boit and Kipkoech (2012) observe that the current push for quantitative standards in the nation's education sector may begin to have counterproductive outcomes. This is especially so considering that funding for higher education essentially comes from the public coffers except in the case of private institutions where tuition fees form the basis of funding (Kinyua, 2020; World Bank, 2019a). For public higher education institutions across the country, funding relies significantly on the government and on international donor agencies (Ooro, 2009; Kauffeldt, 2009). The moves by the Kenyan government to increase tuition fees to consolidate public funding have been met with stiff resistance on the part of students for economic reasons (World Bank, 2019a; McCowan, 2018), which raises vital questions about the sustainability of the government funding for higher education.

According to Koyi et al. (2020), student enrolment in Kenya's tertiary institutions is witnessing a rapid increase, necessitating the establishment of new diversified and specialised institutions to accommodate demand. The World Bank (2019a) observes that while the student population continues to increase, academic staff growth is not commensurate, with only a 13% increase between 2011 and 2018. This challenges the quality and standard of higher education provided by the numerous higher institutions in the country (Maobe & Liping, 2020; World Bank, 2019a).

Recent reports indicate that the Technical and Vocational Education and Training (TVET) institutions in the country currently face problems of inadequate infrastructure due to demographic pressures and access to funding (Mukhwana et al., 2020; World Bank, 2019; McCowan, 2018).

Mulongo (2013) noted that a vast majority of prospective students are unable to access quality education due to the fact that private higher institutions tend to retain qualitative standards in comparison to public higher institutions which are mostly overcrowded and still largely underfunded (Maobe & Liping, 2020; Mulongo, 2013). Of the 40,000 to 60,000 students qualifying for entry into higher education in 2009, Mulongo (2013) observed that only 3% were admitted by private universities while public institutions absorb barely 10%. This was mostly traceable to factors of financial capacity, gender, class, socio-economic elitism, choice of degree, and region of residence. Similarly, Mukhwana et al. (2020) observed a steady decline in the enrolment of students into higher institutions in the country between 2015 and 2019. Thus, although higher education in the country is considerably funded and sponsored by the government, current dynamics underscore the need for more adequate financing and empowerment of higher education in the country to meet qualitative and quantitative needs.

Kenya has a growing research and academic community, with several universities, research institutions and government bodies actively involved in scientific research. Key areas of research in Kenya include agriculture, health, biodiversity, renewable energy, information technology, and social sciences. In terms of research output, Kenya's institutions produced a total of 11,029 publications between 2010 and 2016 (CHET, 2017; Cloete, et al 2018).

Science, technology and research councils in Kenya

The Kenyan government has established a number of councils to help organise and further the inclusion of science technology and innovation research in the country (Ayisi et al., 2019; Fosci et al., 2019; Hanlin, 2017; Ogada et al., 2015; Rugut, 2014). Beginning in 2008 with the introduction of Science, Technology and Innovation Policy, the Kenyan government outlined eight priority research sectors where deliberate attention will be focused to drive its economic growth and attain its national vision. These areas include agriculture, rural development and related industries; health and life sciences; trade and industry; human resource development; physical infrastructure; energy; environmental and natural resource management; and information communication technology (Republic of Kenya Ministry of Science and Technology, 2008). As a result, the National System of Innovation was created to help drive the national vision (Ayisi et al., 2019; Fosci et al., 2019; Hanlin, 2017; Kimenyi et al., 2016). To further re-enact the ideals of the government, the 2013 STI Act was enacted to align STI programmes with national goals and objectives resulting in the creation of four separate bodies to organise STI and research in the country: the National Commission of Science Technology and Innovation (NACOSTI), Advisory Research Committees (ARCs), National Research Fund (NRF) and Kenyan National Innovation Agency (KeNIA) (Ayisi et al., 2019; Fosci et al., 2019; Diyamett et al., 2019).

The NACOSTI acts as the regulator, advisor and coordinator of STI activities in Kenya. The commission also develops national priorities for STI, leads interagency efforts to implement research policies, accredits research institutes and licenses grants to undertake research, makes decisions on funding priorities, develops regulations for research institutes, and monitors the general progress of STI in the country (Fosci et al., 2019; Ayisi et al., 2019; Hanlin, 2017; Edinger & Mackenzie, 2016; Rugut, 2014).

The National Research Fund is saddled with mobilising and managing financial resources for research and development in the country (Ayisi et al., 2019; Ogada et al., 2015; Rugut, 2014). More specifically it is tasked with awarding contracts, grants and scholarships, finances the establishment of research facilities, and supports capacity building across the country (Fosci et al., 2019).

The Kenyan National Innovation Agency manages innovative research mainly for commercialisation by building relationships among and between research and non-research actors, and developing national capacity to develop and disseminate innovation (Fosci et al., 2019; Ayisi et al., 2019; Hanlin, 2017; Edinger & Mackenzie, 2016). Kenya's STI framework and policies have considerably improved the standing of the nation as a major technology hub in the Eastern African region and Africa at large (Diyamett et al., 2019; Edinger & Mackenzie, 2016).

The above policies and initiatives are an attempt to harness the rich research and scientific innovation potentials of the country. As Fosci et al. (2019) observe, there are 14 international research funders and 4 private research funders in the country. The concentration of international corporations and stakeholders in the country puts it in a position to enhance its domestic science technology and innovation sectors especially for socio-economic development (Ayisi et al., 2019; Diyamett et al., 2019; Hanlin, 2017; Edinger & Mackenzie, 2016). The implementation of the various research-enhancing policies and strategies by the government has also significantly improved the standard of university education in the country (Wairegi, 2021; Fosci et al., 2019; Hanlin, 2017).

Through the Universities Act of 2012, the regulation of university education as well as the provision of necessary resources for the enhancing science research in these universities is provided for (Ayisi et al., 2019). The Universities Act established the Commission for University Education, the Universities Funding Board and the Kenya University and Colleges Central Placement Services Board (Ayisi et al., 2019). Through these structures, the government tends to enhance the production of scientific research as well as the dissemination and implementation of these for national development (Wairegi, 2021; Ayisi et al., 2019; Fosci et al., 2019; Hanlin, 2017; Edinger & Mackenzie, 2016). By regulating and funding both private and public universities and research institutes, the country provides a broad spectrum for addressing its socio-economic challenges (Wairegi, 2021; Fosci et al., 2019; Republic of Kenya, 2014).

The Ministry of Education also plays a vital role in promoting and coordinating scientific research in universities across the country (Ayisi et al., 2019). Kenya had a total of 48 universities comprising 22 public universities, 9 public university constituent colleges, 17 chartered private universities, 6 research institutions and 8 commodity research foundations as at 2014 (Ogada et al., 2015). Public universities increased to 31 and private institutions to 30 within a space of seven years; nine of these institutions are among the top 1000 universities globally due to their research performance (Fosci & Loffreda, 2019). The Ministry of Education is also responsible for coordinating STI in the education sector through its four state departments namely, Early Learning and Basic Education; University Education and Research; Technical, Vocational Education and Training (TVET); and the Post Training and Skills Development department (Ayisi et al., 2019).

In relation to the coordination of research and development in universities, the Ministry's State Department for University Education is in charge of departments, parastatals and agencies with mandates to the country' university education (Ayisi et al., 2019). As such, the NACOSTI, NRF and KeNIA reports to the State Department for University Education and Research through the Directorate of Research, Science and Technology (DRST) as far as university education is concerned (Ayisi et al., 2019; Fosci et al., 2019).

This rather complex or central system of managing science research and innovations in academic and research councils ensures that national interests and systems are incorporated into educational processes and research endeavours thus driving national political and economic goals (Ayisi et al., 2019; Fosci et al., 2019; Fosci & Loffreda, 2019; Edinger & Mackenzie, 2016). This level of commitment notwithstanding, the implementation of the goals and recommendations of the STI Act along with other national policies related to science and technology remains below stated expectations in the country even though it is commendable in comparison with its regional neighbours across sub-Saharan Africa (Wairegi, 2021; UNCTAD, 2021; Fosci & Loffreda, 2019; Fosci et al., 2019; Edinger & Mackenzie, 2016).

Coordination of research, science, technology and innovation in Kenya
The coordination of the various science research councils in Kenya while revealing a dedication and appreciation of the government to science technology and innovative research for development, also reveals a very centralised system of organising scientific research in the country (Ayisi et al., 2019; Fosci & Loffreda, 2019; Fosci et al., 2019; Hanlin, 2017; Edinger & Mackenzie, 2016). As revealed in the organised framework of STI and research councils in the nation, the government is responsible for managing and organising research in the country (Ayisi et al., 2019; Fosci & Loffreda, 2019; Republic of Kenya, 2012, 2014, 2015). The government

not only funds but also plays the role of harnessing the various private and public actors in the research and STI sector with very little allowance for science councils to function independently (Ayisi et al., 2019; Fosci et al., 2019; Fosci & Loffreda, 2019). The NACOSTI, KeNIA and NRF are essentially government run and report to the government which gives little room for functioning outside the political aims and allowance of the sitting government (Fosci et al., 2019; Republic of Kenya, 2015/2014/2012; Hanlin, 2017). The Ministry of Education which is also solely responsible for the coordination of education and incorporating STI into academic curriculum and to which the NACOSTI, KeNIA and NRF must report as far as universities and academic institutions are concerned, is also a reflection of the highly centralised system of governance and coordination of STI in the country (Ayisi et al., 2019; Fosci et al., 2019; Republic of Kenya, 2014, 2015).

Science research coordination especially for innovations must necessarily have a level of autonomy to function optimally and which is missing in this case (Fosci & Loffreda, 2019).

One of the major challenges of this largely centralised structure of governing STI and research in Kenya is the fragile nature of the country's political terrain (Mose, 2021; Nyadera et al., 2020; Hanlin, 2017). Due to the nation's political history, there has developed a very fragile political atmosphere especially in times of elections (Wairegi, 2021; Nyadera et al., 2020; Mohajan, 2013). As such, any sudden changes to government or governance as witnessed in previous years could affect STI negatively. Importantly, the key strides and achievements that have been gained in the STI and academic sectors are closely traceable to the concerted efforts of President Uhuru Kenyatta who took over the reins of government in 2013 (Fosci et al., 2019; Hanlin, 2017). Although the 2010 constitution paved the way for the institutionalisation of science and technology and also brought the much-needed balance to the powers of the executive (Mose, 2021; Hanlin, 2017; Mohajan, 2013), the initiation and implementation of STI towards a truly knowledge-driven economy is traceable to the period after 2012 (Fosci et al., 2019; Hanlin, 2017).

The political terrain however remains fragile due to ethnic politics, ethnic rivalry, corruption and power struggles between power blocs in the nation thus making a centralised system of government volatile for socio-economic development (Mose, 2021; Nyadera et al., 2020; Mohajan, 2013). As a result, the country still ranks very low in strength and efficiency of governance structures, and ranks high in terms of the poverty level of citizens (Nyadera et al., 2020; Fosci et al., 2019; Fosci & Loffreda, 2019; Mohajan, 2013). The point therefore is that with exclusively government agencies essentially funding and coordinating scientific research and innovation, with little or no private oversight, there is the fear of unsustainability in driving research.

With governance system that has been acknowledged to be corrupt, the processes and procedures for attracting funding and support for innovative research projects for private institutions and individuals may be susceptible to flaws (Mose, 2021; Fosci & Loffreda, 2019; Hanlin, 2017). Second, the lack of private or non-governmental oversight and/ or partnerships in organising and funding research capabilities in the country may hinder the progressiveness of research as research institutes and councils may be compelled to function only within the aspirations and objectives of the government (Fosci & Loffreda, 2019; Fosci et al., 2019; Hanlin, 2017). This is not an isolated case as Iizuka et al. (2018) and Forson (2017) have shown that African governments are more interested in the science and technology aspects of STI for national development than in the potential of innovation. Although Kenya has proved an exception in this by setting up an innovation agency to oversee the facilitation of innovative research in the country (i.e. KeNIA), the centralisation of this agency in the government raises concerns for the private sector and individual researchers who may not align with government ideals.

In a more liberal and decentralised system, there is increased prospect of healthy competition among researchers and research councils to meet international standards. This is largely missing in the research sector of the country as Fosci and Loffreda (2019) observe that the majority of the researchers do not have a PhD even though there are many think-tanks across the country. Also, most researchers in the country work for the government in public universities making opposition to government policies/ideals difficult (Ayisi et al., 2019; Fosci et al., 2019; Fosci & Loffreda, 2019; Ogada, 2015). The implication of this is that the Kenyan government has systematically hedged in researchers and research institutions under government-controlled agencies so that they are mandated to function within the allowance provided by the government. With such a closed system in organising research, there is hardly opportunity for private organisations and researchers to function without dependence on government (Ayisi et al., 2019; Fosci & Loffreda, 2019; Hanlin, 2017).

There is also the issue of adequate funding for research in the country. Kenya spends 0.8% of its GDP on research and development which is below the 1% recommendation of the Lagos Action Plan but higher than most countries in the African region (Fosci & Loffreda, 2019). Half of its funding however comes from international sources which are mostly managed by the government and disbursed to researchers (Ayisi et al., 2019; Fosci & Loffreda, 2019; Fosci et al., 2019; Hanlin, 2017). The government acts as the intermediary between international granting organisations and private research communities in the country (Fosci & Loffreda, 2019). This has weakened partnerships between the government and private research organisations in the country.

As observed by the government of Kenya, the synergy and network between the various government institutions, research and training institutions, industry, financial sector and professional groups remains weak due to this centralised system (Republic of Kenya, 2015). To pursue a thorough grassroots science research and innovation policy, there is a need to include the private sector into the coordination and implementation of research policies, and to empower private actors to function autonomously without government interference (Fosci & Loffreda, 2019; Fosci et al., 2019; Hanlin, 2017). As reports have shown, the fact that poverty levels across the country continue to increase even with government policies and frameworks aimed at eliminating this trend in place (Wairegi, 2021; Mose, 2021; Nyadera et al., 2020; Fosci & Loffreda, 2019; Mohajan, 2013), indicates the need for deeper levels of grassroot engagements that can only be achieved by the private sector. While the devolution of the country into 47 administrative counties is an important step in decentralising power (Kimenyi et al., 2016), there is need to empower SGCs in the country to function independently of government oversight. This is because the government and government sponsored research councils/agencies are essentially interested in some areas of interests to the detriment of others which may have practical effects at the grassroots level (Fosci & Loffreda, 2019; Iizuka et al., 2018; Forson, 2017). This can be addressed by a diversified and balanced approach to driving STI research in the country.

In conclusion, Kenya's achievements in the STI and research sectors are commendable especially from a country without a specific national

STI policy (Fosci & Loffreda, 2019). As an emerging economy with relatively stable economic growth in the East African region and in sub-Saharan Africa, Kenya stands a chance of attaining STI feats that other nations in the region may find challenging due to socio-political conditions (Fosci & Loffreda, 2019; Fosci et al., 2019). However, like other SGCs in sub-Saharan Africa, the question of coordinating research councils in the country remains a major challenge as the current mode essentially locks out private actors which may be detrimental to the overall attainment of national objectives. The extent to which the private sector is able to pursue its goals independent of government interference determines the level of creativity and innovativeness of the individuals in the country, especially in the STI sector. Therefore, while the current feats in the science and research sectors of the country are laudable, there is a need to enhance private sector participation in coordination and management of STI in the country. The current system amongst its many advantages has the disadvantage of hedging out private interests and organisations from being key players and determinants in the trajectory of scientific research at all levels of society. As it is, the private sector is mostly patronising the resources of the government and not contributing optimally to its development. Consequently, there is need for more funding opportunities, revised legislative options and policies to strengthen private sector capacities in organising and managing the implementation of STI research across the country.

Zambia

Higher education system in Zambia
Higher education in Zambia follows the 7-5-4 structure which means higher education in universities involves four years of study while other technical institutions and vocational training institutes may offer two- or three-year certificate programmes (Moroz, 2016). Advanced educational study programmes such as master's and doctorates generally take a minimum of three to four years (Ministry of Higher Education, 2019; Moroz, 2016). According to Zambia's 2019 National Policy on Education, higher education comprises of all post-secondary school "education, training and research at institutions such as universities, Technical Education, Vocation and Entrepreneurship Training (TEVET) institutions and colleges" (Ministry of Higher Education, 2019).

The academic arm of higher education consists of a Level 6 (diploma certification) grading to a Level 10 (doctorates) grading while the technical and vocational arm of higher education constitutes Level 3 (Certificate) to Level 6 (Diploma) (Ministry of Higher Education, 2019; Moroz, 2016). This allows students to either choose career paths in academic or vocational institutes.

Although the government generally oversees the regulation of education in the country, higher education is highly driven by the private sector. Zambia currently has over 68 universities, 61 of which are private institutions and only 7 public universities. There are 304 technical and vocational (TEVET) colleges, 279 of which are privately owned and 25 public (Kasimba, 2020; Masaiti & Mwale, 2020).

The disparity in access, quality and standards of higher education in the country is observed by scholars and shows a general indisposition to higher education for largely economic reasons (Mukwena, 2021; Higher Education Authority, 2021; Kasimba, 2020). While access to technical, vocational and academic institutions is provided and largely preferred, the Zambia National Policy on Higher Education reported that there was a worryingly low interest in post-secondary school education (Ministry of Higher Education, 2019).

Of all school-leavers in the country, less than 12% are able to access university education due to several factors, particularly funds. Hence there is general preference for TEVET institutions in the country (ZNHEP, 2019). According to the country's Higher Education Authority (2021), private tertiary institutions in Zambia continues to introduce new academic programmes to reflect national and regional needs in terms of knowledge and skills. However, access to these programmes is highly limited because private institutions are essentially smaller, profit-run and funded by relatively higher tuition fees (Higher Education Authority, 2021; Kasimba, 2020; Tamilenthi & Junior, 2011). This presents a unique challenge for the country's socio-economic and socio-political sectors which require high-level skills. Quality assurance and relevance, access and participation in higher education, gender, geographical location as well as efficiency and effectiveness of the various institutions are also concerns associated with the higher education system (Kasimba, 2020; Kunda, Chembe & Mukupa, 2018).

Masaiti and Mwale (2020) for instance observed that some of the unique challenges confronting the Zambian higher education system are the need to improving learner support; the need to design and test new curricula and academic programmes; recruitment; retention; motivation and development of well-trained faculty; enhanced access for disadvantaged students; and enhancing students' basic and applied research capacity.

Public universities in Zambia are particularly noted to lack autonomy, have dilapidated facilities and face general difficulties of imporving access (Masaiti & Mwale, 2020).

Zambia's higher education landscape in recent times have been shaped by internationalisation of education particularly from developed nations like China seeking to establish academic and training institutions in the country (Mukwena, 2021; Masaiti & Mwale, 2020). As Mukwena (2021) observes, while this is a move to improve the overall public sector standard in higher education, there is need to improve the access and affordability of a growing young population to standard private tertiary institutions in the country, especially considering the inability of government funding to cater for growing technical and infrastructural needs in the few public institutions.

The management and regulation of higher education in Zambia until 2013 was handled by the country's Ministry of Education before the Act of Parliament set up the Higher Education Authority to generally provide for quality assurance in university institutions in Zambia (Kasimba, 2020; Ministry of Higher Education, 2019). The Technical Education, Vocational and Entrepreneurship Training Authority (TEVETA) regulates the technical education, vocation and entrepreneurship training institutions while the Zambia Qualification Authority (ZAQA) regulates quality and standards in educational institutions (Masaiti & Mwale, 2020).

The higher education landscape in the country leaves ample opportunity for private individuals and organisations to be active stakeholders in the system, especially in the areas of funding to increase access (particularly for youths in rural areas), research capacity and educational resources in public education institution and facilities.

Zambia has a growing research community with universities, research institutions, and government bodies actively engaged in scientific research. Key areas of research in Zambia include agriculture, health, natural resources, environmental conservation, mining, renewable energy, and social sciences. The Zambia Agricultural Research Institute (ZARI), the National Institute for Scientific and Industrial Research

(NISIR), and the University of Zambia are some of the prominent research institutions in the country. Additionally, the Zambia National Health Research Authority (ZNHRA) plays a significant role in promoting health research and overseeing ethics and quality standards. However, it was difficult to obtain the figures of research output of universities in Zambia. A study by Makondo, et al. (2022) indicates that the University of Zambia had a research output of 516 publications in the year 2018.

Science, technology and research councils in Zambia
Zambia has a number of science technology research councils tasked with driving and managing science research innovations in the country (UNCTAD, 2022; Republic of Zambia, 2017; Republic of Zambia, 1996). The National Science and Technology Council (NSTC) founded in 1997 by the Science Technology Act is the chief body for organising research in the country (UNCTAD, 2022; Sheikheldin, 2018). With a mandate to enhance Zambia's capacity for scientific research and technological development, to create wealth and improve quality of life in the country by promoting the implementation of science and technology, the NSTC began operations in 2000 (UNCTAD, 2022; Sheikheldin, 2018; Republic of Zambia, 2017). The National Council for Scientific Research (NCSR) was previously set up in 1967 to manage scientific research activities but was replaced by the NSTC in 1997 due to some challenges, particularly its statutory limitations with linking other research institutions in the country (UNCTAD, 2022; Republic of Zambia, 2017; Republic of Zambia, 1996). The NCSR was established and mandated to function under the Office of National Development and Planning and was funded by the Venture Capital Fund (UNCTAD, 2022). As a replacement due to its inability to meet national standards and objectives in STI, the NSTC was established (UNCTAD, 2022; Sheikheldin, 2018).

The NSTC has five main functions in the promotion of scientific technology and research in the country which include promotion and advocacy, regulating research in science and technology, advising the government on science and technology related policies, mobilising financial support for science technology research institutions, and coordinating research in science and technology in Zambia (UNCTAD, 2022; Sheikheldin, 2018; Republic of Zambia, 2017). In pursuant of its roles in enhancing scientific research in the country, the NSTC partners with several domestic councils and agencies of government such as the

National Research Fund, the University of Zambia, the National Remote Sensing Centre (NRSC), the National Technology Business Centre, the Copperbelt University, Zambia Information and Communications Technology Authority (ZICTA), Zambia Agricultural Research Institute, National Institute for Scientific and Industrial Research (NISIR), the Technology Development and Advisory Unit (TDAU), the Central Veterinary Research Institute (CVRI), The National Malaria Control Centre (NMCC), Junior Engineers, Technicians and Scientists (JETS), the Engineering Institution of Zambia (EIZ), the Ministry of Higher Education and other government industries and ministries (Sheikheldin, 2018).

Three other government-owned science councils were set up by the Science and Technology Act of 1997: the National Institute for Scientific and Industrial Research (NISIR), the National Technology Business Centre (NTBC), and the National Remote Sensing Centre (NRSC) (UNCTAD, 2022; Sheikheldin, 2018; Republic of Zambia, 2017). These agencies have their various specific roles and responsibilities in the enhancement of science and technology in the country although they also share responsibilities (Republic of Zambia, 2017). The NISIR for instance replaced the former National Remote Sensing Centre (NRSC) which was established in 1999 to deal with remote sensing and geographic information systems technologies (UNCTAD, 2022). The NISIR inherited the mandate of the NRSC and continued to function under the Ministry of Higher Education until it was replaced in the country's new 2020 STI Policy by the Ministry of Science and Technology (UNCTAD, 2022). The National Technology Business Centre is tasked with commercialising research technologies and innovations for the benefit of entrepreneurs and business communities as well as managing a proposed venture capital fund (UNCTAD, 2022; Republic of Zambia, 2017). Prior to the establishment of a new STI Policy, the three institutions were governed by departments in the Ministry of Education but have now been moved to the Ministry of Science and Technology since the initiation of the 2020 National STI Policy (UNCTAD, 2022; Republic of Zambia, 2017).

In the health sector, Zambia established the National Health Research Authority in 2013 through the National Health Research Act of 2013 (UNCTAD, 2022; Republic of Zambia, 2017). The Authority is responsible for the enhancement of health-related research in the country while also promoting patent rights and intellectual property (UNCTAD, 2022).

The institutional framework for the organisation and regulation of science research in the country according to the structure outlined above lie mostly with the government through its academic and STI ministries (Sheikheldin, 2018). Though the various research institutes and councils have their specific functions through which they promote the advancement of research in the country, there is robust partnership between them that helps to leverage their strengths and capacities (UNCTAD, 2022; Sheikheldin, 2018; Republic of Zambia, 2017). This partnership however ensures that government is solely in charge of funding, initiating, developing, managing, regulating, and commercialising technological innovations in the country (UNCTAD, 2022; Sheikheldin, 2018; UNECA, 2014).

Due to the centralised system of organising science research in the country, UNECA (2014) observed that 66% of research funding comes from the government while 42% originates from donors.

Coordination of research, science, technology and innovation in Zambia
The coordination of research, science and technology innovations as revealed in the above structure lies entirely with the government (UNCTAD, 2022; Sheikheldin, 2018; UNECA, 2014). Science governing councils in the country are not self-reliant but heavily dependent on external bodies for funding and functioning (UNECA, 2014). While there is partnership between the various organisations, the NSTC coordinates and oversees science and research activities in Zambia (UNCTAD, 2022). The private sector is mostly relegated to a minimal role which as Bolo (2020) rightly observes reduces the chances for creativity, accessing funds, and developing research infrastructures within the research industry. With such a closed system, the challenges bedevilling the government's agencies and institutions would ordinarily hinder the successful implementation of the country's STI policies. An indication of the inability of the current system of coordination and regulation to meet the needs of the country in terms of scientific and technological development is the continual underdevelopment of the country's socio-political and socio-economic sector (UNCTAD, 2022; Bertelsmann Stiftung, 2020; Chikalipah & Manika, 2019). Also, the huge reliance on public funds not only undermines access to sufficient funds but also limits the overall capacity of the various science granting councils to function optimally (UNCTAD, 2022; Bertelsmann Stiftung, 2020; Republic of Zambia, 2017; UNECA, 2014).

Furthermore, due to the country's reliance on copper, other research areas in the country hardly attract the required support needed to sponsor diverse research especially in the education, information technology, agricultural and health sectors are lacking (Chikalipah & Manika, 2019; UNECA, 2014; African Economic Outlook, 2012; DiJohn, 2010). The establishment of the Copperbelt University is proof of Zambia's bias for research in that area while the other important sectors like health and education continue to lag in the number of investments and infrastructure dedicated for the purpose (UNCTAD, 2022). The problem of poor research capacities in the nation is also evident in the biased historical narrative of the country's political development by some political researchers (DiJohn, 2010; Larmer, 2006). This tendency shows that the government and government-sponsored researchers and agencies may not be trusted for objective research for national growth and development (Fedderke et al., 2011; Larmer, 2006). However, since the nation's independence and first government, this tendency to control the narrative of development in all areas of research has led to an organisational structure that essentially excludes the private sector and promotes government activities which as practical results have shown is not sufficient for achieving the country's sustainable development goals (Bertelsmann Stiftung, 2020; UNECA, 2014; African Economic Outlook, 2012).

Zambia's research and academic institutions, like other public institutions, tend to function less optimally than expected due to the limited capacity and institutional corruption that has hindered the ease of doing business in the country (UNCTAD, 2022; Bertelsmann Stiftung, 2020; Chikalipah & Manika, 2019). The country for instance ranked 87th in the World Bank's 2019 Ease of Doing Business Report and also ranked 102 out of 190 in "Starting a Business" index (UNCTAD, 2022). Economic freedom has also consistently declined from 88th in 2015 to 138th in 2019 according to Heritage Foundation Index of Economic Freedom (UNCTAD, 2022). The implication of this in the country's economic sector is that for government-controlled SGC councils like the NBTC which is supposed to lead the commercialisation of science and technology innovations, a poor business sector indirectly hinders its work. This is complicated by the fact that the private sector is not empowered enough to play an active role in driving science and technology innovations (UNECA, 2014). The Bertelsmann Stiftung's 2020 report indicates that dissenting views from various actors other than the government are generally threatened and squashed by the government and its agencies even in the case of public universities (Bertelsmann Stiftung, 2020). In such an environment, private enterprises and institutions are hardly encouraged to thrive because they are not treated as partners in progress.

There is also the issue of funding to cover the demands and requirements of the various science granting councils in the country (Bertelsmann Stiftung, 2020; Republic of Zambia, 2017; UNECA, 2014). With less than 4% of its GDP committed to education and health, the country's education sector which is essentially supposed to drive the implementation of Zambia's STI and research policies along with the Ministry of Science and Technology, is grossly underfunded (UNECA, 2014). In December 2018, for instance, the government refused to pay students' meal allowances, and this resulted in mass protests by students that led to the death of a student (Bertelsmann Stiftung, 2020). The government further announced in January 2019 that it would no longer pay these allowances to students due essentially to poor economic conditions which no doubt negatively affect the overall development of education in the country (Bertelsmann Stiftung, 2020). While the organisational framework for addressing science and technology research is provided for by the government, the financial capacity to implement this is waning since the government remains the largest financial sponsor of STI in the country (UNCTAD, 2022; Sheikheldin, 2018; UNECA, 2014). As a UN study reports, the quality of education continues to decline in the country along with access to basic education (UNCTAD, 2022). While 84% of children in Zambia attend primary school with a completion rate of 70%, reports show that this rate drops further to 50% in secondary school and 27% for upper schools (UNCTAD, 2022).

The problem therefore with the funding, equipping and enhancement of science technology and innovation research in Zambia has less to do with the availability of policy framework but more to do with partnership with the private sector and commitment to financial integrity by the government (UNCTAD, 2022; Bertelsmann Stiftung, 2020; Sheikheldin, 2018). Aside from the need to build synergy with the private sector to ensure an autonomous private science research community in the country, the dwindling inflow of funds especially from donor governments and organisations are red flags that must be addressed (Bertelsmann Stiftung, 2020; UNECA, 2014). This unstable inflow of funds due to the mismanagement of public funds does not help the growth of science and technology research in the country since most donor governments and agencies are withdrawing their aid to the country (Bertelsmann Stiftung, 2020). Building a formidable science and technology research sector must therefore leverage on both the private and public sectors and this must necessarily involve building up private sector capacity to coordinate and fund research capabilities in the country (Sheikheldin, 2018). This is important for SGCs in Zambia to promote healthy competition and professionalism required to attain global standards in scientific research. More importantly, such empowerment is likely to enhance the attainment of the country's national vision 2030 if pursued adequately. The partnership with international governments and organisations is a relationship that could be leveraged upon to build private sector capacities for national growth.

Science granting councils in South Africa

South Africa has been adjudged to have a well-developed science and technology infrastructure needed for research and innovation to thrive. This is evident in its scientific publication and patenting record which makes it the leading country in terms of research and innovation in Africa (Patra & Muchie, 2018). Therefore, South Africa has been chosen as a point of reference because of its strides in research and innovation which makes it the leading country on the continent of Africa. Its higher education system, and its robust science, technology and innovation structure alongside its control, coordinating and its funding system, are deemed important for other African states to learn from and to improve their existing models in terms of research and innovation, as well as funding for improved research. On the other hand, various challenges encountered in the process of improving and consolidating its research and innovation infrastructure are also discussed for a balanced and well-informed account of an existing system vis-à-vis science, technology and innovation in South Africa.

The higher education system in South Africa
South Africa runs a three-tier education system comprising primary, secondary and tertiary in a 9-3-3 system (Berg & Helmeyr, 2018). In 2021, the Post-School Education and Training system had 342 institutions,

namely: 26 public universities, 124 private higher education Institutions, 50 technical and vocational education and training (TVET) colleges, 133 registered private colleges, and 9 community education and training (CET) colleges (Department of Higher Education and Training, 2023). The University of South Africa (Unisa) is the country's largest university offering distance learning programmes (Ariail, 2016).

Prior to 1994, the higher education system was largely polarised and disintegrated by racial discrimination which reserved certain universities for whites in urban areas and others for blacks in Bantustan areas (Gore & Walker, 2020; Berg & Hofmeyr, 2018). This system largely saw the education of a limited number of Black South Africans while also considerably limiting academic curricula to reflect apartheid and racially discriminating political systems. Following democratic reforms, the National Commission on Higher Education (NCHE) was established in 1995 to oversee the coordination of higher education. It was tasked with establishing a non-racial higher education system for the country (Moja & Cloete, 1996). Educational reforms were put in place that not only integrated multiple higher education systems but also facilitated the access and acquisition of higher education through systematic funding and scholarship schemes (Berg & Hofmeyr, 2018; Archer, 2017). The National Student Financial Aid Scheme (NSFAS) established in 1991 provides financial support for students from low-income families. As at 2015, the scheme had funded students to the tune of ZAR 7.2 billion (Berg & Hofmeyr, 2018). Those reforms led to the enrolment of over 1 million university students in 2016 from less than 500,000 in 1994 (UNECA, 2017).

The Department of Higher Education and Training (DHET) is responsible for tertiary education in the country and has consistently attracted larger budgets from the government of South Afica to fund education of students from low-income families (Bertelsmann Stiftung Index, 2022). Certain challenges and structures implicative of the apartheid regime continue to exist in the higher education landscape in the country as evident in the disparity in quality of staff and gender distribution among students (Gore & Walker, 2020; Archer, 2017; Public Servants' Association, 2016). The Public Servants' Association (2016) observes that employability for graduates of universities in South Africa is highly influenced by the quality of university attended, citing that formerly whites-only universities in the country possess better teaching and qualitative staff than their formerly blacks-only counterparts.

Furthermore, while higher education has been opened to all, statistics indicate that more females than males are enrolled in all but three universities in the country (Archer, 2017; Public Servants' Association, 2016). Also, the quality of the performance of students of various racial classifications across the universities has reportedly been influenced by the extended racialisation of higher education. According to Berg and Hofmeyr (2018), the quality of student academic performance and eventual graduation is evident from data on time-to-degree in the country where three- or four-year courses can take up to six years to complete.

Research and innovation in South Africa is largely powered by its higher education system (Mouton et al., 2018) which has profited considerably from government funding as well as the tuition fees paid by students (Ariail, 2017; Public Servants' Association, 2016; Lefa, 2014). This system helps to improve the quality of tertiary education by supporting staff recruitment, research and innovation funding, which is has not been the case in low-income countries (Berg & Hofmeyr, 2018).

The 2015 protests to reduce university fees for low-income students is an indicator of the need for more higher education funding (Public Servants' Association, 2016). The point however is that the quality of higher education in South Africa is not solely tied to governance and funding from government, but also to funding that is gained, specifically through tuition fees. Universities that rank in the global universities rankings are universities that combine both public and private sources of financing to improve the quality of staff, students, research capacity and the learning environment. The strides made by universities in science, technology and innovation can be attributed largely to consistent government funding and high student fees.

South African universities are generally respected in the African region and beyond for their technological innovation and research with several of its universities ranking amongst top universities in the world (Ariail, 2016; PSA, 2016). The Center for World University Rankings for 2014 included four South African universities among its top 500 global universities with no other African university represented. The QS World University Rankings for 2014–2015 also included four South African universities in its top 500 universities ranking, while the Shanghai Academic Rankings of World Universities included five South African universities amongst its top 500 universities (Ariail, 2016). The

2023 ranking by Times Higher Education indicates that South African universities took the first three positions in Africa,[3] which further shows the leading role South Africa's higher education system plays on the continent.

According to Patra and Muchie (2018), universities in South Africa produced 91% of the total academic publications in the country and for a total of 14% of patents for the country. There has been an increase from 7,230 publication units in 2005 to 21,019 in 2019 (Sebola, 2023). In 2020, 21,734.3 units were recorded while in 2022, publications increased to 23,416.32 units.[4] This indicates increasing productivity on the part of public universities in South Africa. This equally explains why South African universities take the leading role in Africa. It is important to reiterate that the South African government introduced the Research Output Policy in 2005 to "encourage research productivity by rewarding quality research outputs at public higher education institutions" (Department of Higher Education and Training, 2021, 3). Research production is also incentivised by giving financial rewards for publications to universities. This could partially explain why South Africa has a higher record of published works compared with other public universities on the continent.

The major science technology and research councils in South Africa are discussed in the next section.

Science, technology and research councils in South Africa
The National System for Innovation (NSI) approach to development was adopted in 1996 by the South African government and outlined in the White Paper on Science and Technology (Republic of South Africa, 2019; Department of Science and Technology, 2018; UNECA, 2017; Raphasha, 2015). It equally laid the foundation for the establishment of National Research Foundation (NRF) through the National Research Foundation Act (No. 23 of 1998). By adopting the NSI, the country became the first in Africa to adopt a national system for innovation (UNSA, 2020; UNECA, 2017). The NSI aimed at the implementation of science, technology

---

3   https://www.timeshighereducation.com/student/best-universities/
     best-universities-africa
4   Report on the Evaluation of the 2021 Universities' Research Outputs. Published March
     2023

and innovation to drive development in the country (Republic of South Africa, 2019; Raphasha, 2015). The Department of Arts, Culture, Science and Technology (DACST) was initially responsible for administering the newly adopted NSI although other government agencies and organs played significant oversight roles (UNCTAD, 2021; Department of Science and Technology, 2018; UNECA, 2017; Raphasha, 2015). The DACST was later renamed to become the Department of Science and Technology (DST) for a more structured and narrow commitment to science and technology innovation in the country (Raphasha, 2015; Moses et al., 2012). The DST has since been renamed the Department of Science and Innovation (DSI) and the NRF reports to and is funded by the DSI. Other structures involved include the Parliamentary Portfolio Committee for STI which comprises members of parliament and provides an oversight function of the Department of Science and Innovation and its constituent agencies. This is a structure consisting of politically elected officials who play a role in giving direction and trajectory of the DSI.

The National Planning Commission (NPC) and the Department of Performance Monitoring and Evaluation (DPME) provide "high-level policy framework for strategic guidance and accountability" for the DSI (Raphasha, 2015). While the DSI is therefore saddled with designing innovation policy, and developing and implementing these policies in South Africa, the NPC and DPME monitor the DSI in providing such functions (UNECA, 2017; Raphasha, 2015; Moses et al., 2012). The DSI has drafted several policies in line with its mandate over the years such as the National Research and Technology Foresight (1999); the National Research and Development Strategy (2002); the Ten-Year Innovation Plan (TYIP); the Innovation Towards a Knowledge-Based Economy 2008–2018; the Science, Technology and Innovation Decadal Plan 2008–2018; and the 2022 Science, Technology and Innovation Decadal Plan amongst others (Department of Science and Innovation, 2022; Department of Science and Technology, 2018; Raphasha, 2015). Through these policies and its agencies which have been established over the years, the DSI essentially develops, finances and coordinates science and technology research in the country (Department of Science and Technology, 2018; Raphasha, 2015; Moses et al., 2012).

There are other key role players such as the Academy of Science of South Africa (ASSAf), Council for Scientific and Industrial Research (CSIR), Human Sciences Research Council (HSRC), South African

Council for Natural Scientific Professions (SACNASP). Other science and research bodies include, South African Bureau of Standards (SABS), National Intellectual Property Management Office (NIPMO), Agricultural Research Council (ARC), Mintek (Mineral resources), Council for Geoscience (CGS), South African Medical Research Council (SAMRC), National Health Laboratory Service (NHLS), South African National Energy Development Institute (SANEDI), Water Research Commission (WRC), South African Environmental Observation Network (SAEON), South African Astronomical Observatory (SAAO).[5] The above is a reflection that the DSI recognises the importance of all sectors towards to realisation of the NSI mandate. These agencies all have their mandates, performance indicators, agreements and governance bodies appointed by the DSI and the government (APRE, 2015; Raphasha, 2015).

Other key government agencies that play significant role in the implementation of the NSI are the Department of Trade Industry and Competition which is a major funder of technology research and innovation in the country (Raphasha, 2015). The Economic Development Department (EDD) was established in 2009 with a mandate to promote economic development through participatory, coherent and coordinated economic policy and planning for the benefit of all South Africans (Department for Business, Energy & Industrial Strategy, 2022; Raphasha, 2015). The EDD plays a significant role in NSI by overseeing the Industrial Development Cooperation (IDC) which manages the Support Programme for Industrial Innovation that are key drivers of science and innovation in the private sector (APRE, 2015; Raphasha, 2015). The National Advisory Council on Innovation (NACI) established in 1998 is also a government body that provides advisory functions on NSI to the Minister of Higher Education, Science and Innovation (Department for Business, Energy & Industrial Strategy, 2022). The body reports directly to the Minister of Higher Education, Science and Innovation for which it provides advisory functions thus limiting access to other NSI government departments (Raphasha, 2015). Thus, although the NACI is set up to provide advisory functions, the powers of this body to influence major DSI decisions and steer programmes are limited.

---

5   https://www.gov.za/about-sa/science-technology

In 2008, the NACI was reviewed with the purpose of making it a national body in the President's Office that provided high-level steerage for NSI agencies thus making it a key player in the science research and innovation sector (Raphasha, 2015). However, in 2015 a report indicated that the organisation had not been able to gain visibility in terms of profiling its work and does not have the capacity to influence actors in the NSI especially due to its structure, position and limited powers to carry out its functions (Raphasha, 2015).

This structural diversification of South Africa's NSI governing councils have made it difficult to successfully implement a coordinated national science innovation system across the country (Tigabu & Khaemba, 2020; Mouton et al., 2019; African Technology Policy Studies Network, 2020). As Raphasha (2015) has argued, both the DSI and the NACI

> have not been able to coordinate and manage the process of designating the fragmented and diversified NSI as coordinators. As a result, South Africa's NSI continues to be inadequate at both the vertical (across different levels of government) and horizontal (across government departments) integration of purpose and effort amongst the actors in the NSI). The limited integration and coherence is reflected in many of the misaligned policies, strategies and institutions; and R&D activities appear to be highly fragmented and not result in commercial marketable value. (Raphasha, 2015, 36)

Bailey (2020) equally identified some of these flaws and recommended an improvement in the internal capacity, independence, profile and credibility of NACI as well as clarity in the roles of both NACI and the DSI. This study could not ascertain to what extent changes have been made to the existing coordinating structure.

Private institutions and civil society also play significant roles in science research and technological innovations in the country (Mouton et al., 2019; UNECA, 2017; Raphasha, 2015). While the government in all its public departments on innovation and science research includes private sector organisations as strategic partners in the NSI implementation system, there are no independent private science agencies without government influence (Tigabu & Khaemba, 2020; Department of Science and Technology, 2018; Mouton et al., 2014). The fragmented nature of the various bodies and councils responsible for implementing innovative research in the country remains a source of concern (Raphasha, 2015; Moses et al., 2012). The implications of this fragmented and seemingly uncoordinated approach to organising science research have had dire consequences on the implementation of science innovation at the grassroots level (UNECA, 2017; Raphasha, 2015; Moses et al., 2012).

Coordination of research, science, technology and innovation in South Africa
From the above indications, the South African government is largely responsible for the organising, coordination, funding, monitoring and implementation of science and innovation technologies through its NSI (Republic of South Africa, 2019; UNSA, 2020; Department of Science and Technology, 2018; UNECA, 2017). For a diversified economy, such unilateral and central approach to science and technology research governance in the country may be subject to undesirable consequences. For instance, due to the solely public approach to the organisation and coordination of NSI in the country, private research firms and institutes are restrained by government's political agenda and objectives (Tigabu & Khaemba, 2020; Mouton et al., 2019). Also, with a background of weak public institutions, reliance on government agencies like the NACI to play advisory roles have been reported to be nonexistent, especially because they are not structurally equipped for the assignment (Raphasha, 2015). Furthermore, the exclusion of the private and non-government agencies and players in the coordination of research activities in South Africa has negatively hampered the grassroots effects of research findings and innovation technologies (Tigabu & Khaemba, 2020; Raphasha, 2015; UNECA, 2017). Reporting on the state of academic institutions at the basic education level on science and mathematics, UNECA (2017) observed that South African schools are generally of low quality even though the DSI through its numerous departments and agencies is supposed to implement and see to the quality of science subjects at all levels of education in the country.

Amongst the implications of government-driven coordination of science and technology research in the country is the limitation of individual potential in promoting a technological society (ATPS, 2020; UNECA, 2017). Although South Africa has been noted to be a contributor of new science and technological innovations, the rate of unemployment and lack of access to necessary finance to undertake projects outside of government interests also remains a concern (African Technology Policy Studies Network, 2020). This has been reported to be a problem for SGCs in the country because dependence on the government means private research bodies and agencies streamline their innovative activities and objectives to government interests (Tigabu & Khaemba, 2020; Mouton et al., 2019; Chataway et al., 2017). Similarly, dependence on foreign aid also means SGCs in the country have to adopt international research areas of interests to attract funds for research (Tigabu & Khaemba, 2020).

Insights from South Africa for African SGCs
The situation described above thrives on the lack of empowerment for private research agencies to operate independently of government aid. And this has been recognised as a leading challenge of SGCs in sub-Saharan Africa (ATPS, 2020). The overwhelming dependence on the government for funds and monitoring has a track record of negatively affecting the objectivity of science research in countries (ATPS, 2020; Tigabu & Khaemba, 2020; Mouton et al., 2019; Mouton & Astrid, 2017).

Partnerships with the private sector therefore actually do not empower SGCs to function with their own goals and objectives which can drive national innovation and enhance quality, particularly in academic research (Tigabu & Khaemba, 2020; Chataway et al., 2017). Instead, partnerships are avenues to incorporate the private research and science councils into serving government goals and objectives and not necessarily to drive a diversified research community (Mouton et al. 2015). As Chataway et al. (2017) state, researchers across sub-Saharan Africa have difficulties accessing funds for projects that have to do with local domestic concerns and even in cases when such projects are executed, there is difficulty in recognising these works at the national level.

Furthermore, decision-making relating to areas of priority for national research and innovation are exclusively decided by government bodies and by implication government actors (Tigabu & Khaemba, 2020; ATPS, 2020; Chataway et al., 2017). This essentially excludes the private sector from important decision-making processes. The current organisation and framing of SGCs across Africa follows this unilateral and central system and this may very well be responsible for the lack of practical implication of research and innovation advancements for grassroots populations both in South Africa and across Africa.

Based on the literature explored, we observe that though the government of South Africa partners with the private sector to generate more funding for research activities in the country, there is a disconnect between the government and the role the private sector could play with regard to the coordination processes of research and innovation, as well as the process of setting government research priorities in the country. This is where the NRF's intervention is timely as it aims to bridge this gap between the government and the industry in all spheres by harnessing all of the private sectors' potentials vis-a-vis research and innovation in South Africa.

In 2019, the NRF came up with the NRF Industry Partnership Strategy to address this disconnect by "supporting, promoting and advancing research and human capacity development to facilitate the creation of knowledge, innovation and development in order to contribute to national development" (National Research Foundation, 2019, 3). The strategy focuses on innovative research and human capacity development by mobilising the private sector and state-owned enterprises with the ultimate goal of building long-term relationships between industry and academia, and the NRF.

Equally, through this strategy, the NRF aims to pay attention to industry and societal needs through the co-creation of research activities and the exchange of ideas between universities and industry through platforms created to facilitate access to technology, information and human resources.

In addition, this partnership aligns with the White Paper on Science, Technology and Innovation which emphasises the importance of government–industry partnerships towards national development. This is an important strategy adopted by the NRF which other countries could consider on the continent to enhance and accelerate the generation of knowledge to address societal needs and, in turn, the development of the country.

Conclusion

This chapter has shown the disparate higher education systems in the selected countries and patterned from the education systems of their former colonial masters. It has also shown the disparate commitment that manifest in varying measures towards the building of a functional system of education and the implementation of the varying policies aimed at improving the education system in each country. Over the years, these systems have been subjected to varying reforms in terms of functionality, control and coordination. This indicates the interest of countries towards having an education system, especially at the higher education level, that produces individuals with the needed skills for research and innovation activities and who will, in turn contribute to development.

However, what we have seen at the various national levels is far from the required result. A major assumption made in the improvement and consolidation of the various science and higher education systems is that funding is available for the implementation of the relevant policies. This is an area where South Africa stands out on the continent in terms of its research and innovation structure which makes it possible for universities and research institutions to be productive in terms of research output (academic publications and inventions). So far, the country has been able to fund its higher education through joint partnership between the government and industry which has enhanced and further deepened the realisation of the NSI in the country. This is manifested in the research output of universities and research institutions in South Africa.

It is important to note that the introduction of the 2005 Research Output Policy in South Africa has no doubt yielded positive result in terms of publication output. Perhaps, there is a lesson for other African countries to learn from here, while also acknowledging the dangers inherent in an incentive scheme that provides financial reward for publication outputs (Mouton & Valentine, 2018). Such a scheme requires funding at a level which the governments of many African states have over the years shown that they are not capable of providing. Therefore, it becomes imperative for governments of African states to come to a realisation that they cannot singlehandedly fund higher education and research in their respective countries and recognise the role the private sector can play in the improvement of their higher education and science systems. Industry should be considered as partners in progress for the NSI approach to development to be achievable at national levels across all African states.

A Study of Governance and Funding of African Science Granting Councils

Empirical Findings

The findings from this study covers areas such as how SGCs are structured, organised and funded; what evidence exists of progress being made towards linking research to development, innovation, and the valorisation of research products; partnering with the private sector; and ways to unlock additional funding for scientific research. Since the study took place during the Covid-19 pandemic, we added a component of understanding the challenges SGCs were facing during the pandemic and how they have managed to develop coping strategies

Science granting council structures

African governments have, through the African Union, established AUDA–NEPAD as a development agency to coordinate and execute priority regional development projects.[6] This is a structure operating at a regional level, while SGCs operate at a national level, thus requiring a certain degree of coordination. The SGCs serve as intermediary agencies between governments and research institutions. Currently, the SGCs are at different development stages in terms of them operating as independent agencies or being located within a government ministry. Of the four countries chosen for the study – Kenya, Zambia, and Côte d'Ivoire – have well-established SGC's, while Botswana's operates as part of the Ministry of Tertiary Education, Research, Science, and Technology. Table 3 compares the similarities and differences that exist amongst the governance structures and functions of the four SGCs participating in this study.

TABLE 3 Governance structures of the SGCs in Botswana, Côte d'Ivoire, Kenya and Zambia

SCIENCE GRANTING COUNCIL	MINISTRY	FUNCTIONS	DIVISIONS/UNITS	COORDINATION
BOTSWANA The Department of Research, Science and Technology (DRST)	Ministry of Tertiary Education, Research, Science and Technology	Coordinates research, technology and innovation in Botswana.	Two units: Coordination and Development Unit and Monitoring and Evaluation (M&E) Unit. Both units headed by Chief Research and Technology Officers.	Headed by a Director who reports to the Deputy Permanent Secretary (DPS) in the Ministry. The DPS reports to the Chair or Permanent Secretary (PS) of the Ministry. The PS reports to Cabinet or to the Minister (who reports to Cabinet).
CÔTE D'IVOIRE Strategic Support for Scientific Research Programme (PASRES)	Ministry of Higher Education and Scientific Research	Coordinates all research and innovation activities in the country.	Three units: Steering Committee, Scientific Council, and Executive Secretariat.	Headed by an Executive Secretary who oversees the activities of the three units.
KENYA The National Research Fund (NRF)	Ministry of Education, Science and Technology	Supports the advancement of scientific research, inventions and innovations and the building of capacity in STI. Provides funds for policy-oriented research as determined in the government development targets – the Big Four Agenda.	One of three institutions established through the STI Act of 2013: NACOSTI, NRF, and KeNIA.	NACOSTI, NRF and KeNIA are each headed by a CEO. The three work hand-in-hand in the performance of their unique duties. Representatives of each of the three institutions sit on each other's boards and they all have a say in the formulation and implementation of research activities

---

6   https://www.nepad.org/who-we-are/about-us

SCIENCE GRANTING COUNCIL	MINISTRY	FUNCTIONS	DIVISIONS/UNITS	COORDINATION
ZAMBIA The National Science and Technology Council (NSTC)	Ministry of Technology and Science	Statutory mandate: promote STI for improved quality of life in Zambia. This mandate is fulfilled through four functional pillars: (i) promotion and advocacy, (ii) regulation and coordination, (iii) resource mobilisation and disbursement, and (iv) policy advising.	Divided into Programme Development and Implementation, and Administration and Finance.	The Council is headed by a Chair who is the administrative head of the NSTC. The CEO (Head of Secretariat) reports to the Council, which in turn reports to the Minister as provided for in the Act. The CEO also has regular interactions with officials from the Ministry.

Science granting council in Botswana

Botswana is the only country included where SGC functions are performed by a government department located in the Ministry of Tertiary Education, Research, Science and Technology (DRST) (see Table 3). We have classified the DRST as a non-autonomous agency, as it functions as an extended arm of government supporting research activities, dispersing research funds and ensuring that government research priorities are addressed. The DRST has a mandate to create a conducive environment for research and innovation to take place, and to coordinate STI activities. This is done primarily through the development of research, science, technology, and innovation (RSTI) policies, development of policy instruments, as well as initiatives to engage the public and engage other stakeholders in RSTI. Furthermore, the DRST is responsible for capacity building and promoting the inclusion of women in research. In terms of structure, the DRST reports to its parent ministry and is headed by a director who reports to the Deputy-Permanent Secretary (DPS) in the Ministry; the DPS reports to the Permanent Secretary (PS).

The core of the DRST consists of about 10 personnel, including the Director and Deputy-Director. It is divided into two divisions headed by Chief Research and Technology Officers. As shown in Figure 2, the first division is charged with the responsibility of coordination and development, while the other is charged with responsibilities related to policy and legislation.

Each division is headed by a Chief Research and Technology officer. The first division is composed of three core units: M&E; Database Management; and Science, Information and Technology. The second division is composed of Policy Development and Legislation, Forecasting and Planning, and Intellectual Property Protection. The three units in each of the two divisions function as a single unit, with only one staff member overseeing the affairs of each. Other administrative staff members are responsible for finances, human resources, transport, and operations.

There are challenges with the coordination of activities, as different ministries continue to report through their own channels. Botswana is in a transitional phase, with ongoing discussions regarding the establishment of a research fund and the transformation of the current research-related government structures such that they are positioned under one directorate. The National Policy on Research, Science, Technology, and Innovation proposes that a Botswana National Research, Development, and Innovation Coordinating Council be established to advise the leadership of the country and coordinate decision-making on RSTI issues. This Council would be established by statute and function as an autonomous body chaired by the Minister responsible for Science and Technology. This Council is yet to be established.

There are several other committees that have been constituted to facilitate coordination and interactions between the DRST and research units in other ministries. One of these is the Zonal Joint Committee, which serves as a platform for discussing progress within national and regional research projects in the country. A monitoring and evaluation (M&E) framework, which was adopted after consultations with a broad range of stakeholder, was developed to strengthen coordination efforts in the country.

Another entity is the Botswana Joint Committee (BJC) on Science and Technology – initially established to manage its relationship with primarily South Africa. Over time, the BJC has been commissioned to coordinate activities that are science and technology related amongst different institutions within the country. It is composed of representatives from various ministries and organisations and chaired by the DPS for the Ministry of Tertiary Education, Research, Science, and Technology. The BJC holds meetings quarterly, where reports and updates on ongoing projects are shared, challenges can be discussed, and solutions jointly developed. Whatever is decided at this level is reported to the ministries, which then report to the national government.

In the course of the present study, the DPS acknowledged in one of our meetings that Botswana has benefitted from participating in the

FIGURE 2 Organisational structure of the Department of Research, Science and Technology (DRST), Botswana

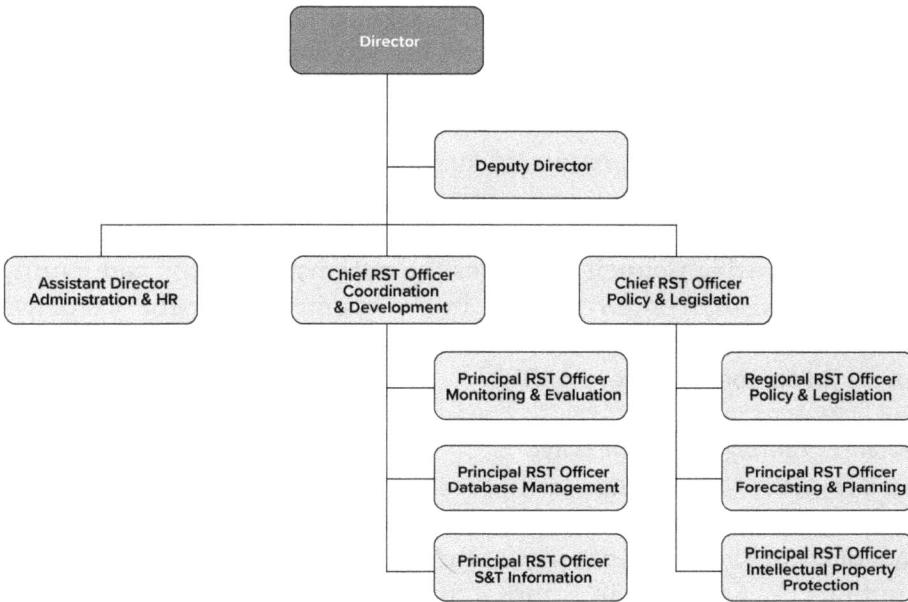

Source: DRST Botswana 2021 (As provided by DRST)

SGCI and that it has helped them with their capacity-building efforts. It was further stated that they have gained knowledge on the operation of an independent SGC. As part of the steps towards the establishment of an independent SGC, Botswana has been studying other models and structures such as the South African NRF and the African Academy of Sciences. The latter operates on a lean but effective structure, which is of particular interest to the DRST.

Science granting council in Côte d'Ivoire

Côte d'Ivoire has an independent SGC, the Strategic Support for Scientific Research Programme (*Programme d'Appui Strategique a la Recherche Scientifique*) or PASRES. It was established after Côte d'Ivoire and Switzerland signed a scientific cooperation agreement in 2006. As shown in Table 3, PASRES consists of three bodies: the Steering Committee, the Scientific Council, and the Executive Secretariat. The Steering Committee is the apex body of the organisation, giving direction to the other two in terms of priorities at the sub-regional (e.g., Economic Community of West African States) and national level. The Steering Committee interacts with the political community, policy-makers, and private sector, and it is composed of representatives from the Ministry of Higher Education and Scientific Research as well as the private sector. The participation of the private sector is key, given that many governments in Africa cannot adequately provide the resources for scientific research and innovation. This is why Côte d'Ivoire sees the private sector as key to the mobilisation of funding for scientific research.

The Scientific Council mobilises the national scientific community and legitimises PASRES' mission in the country, while the Executive Secretariat (headed by the Executive Secretary) oversees the activities of all three bodies under PASRES.

Science granting council in Kenya
In Kenya, the National Science and Technology Innovation Centre (NSTIC) was established under the National Science, Technology and Innovation Act of 2013. The NSTIC consists of three institutions: NACOSTI, the NRF, and KeNIA. As shown in Figure 3, the NRF is the SGC and the agency that provides funding for research. As is the case with Côte d'Ivoire and Zambia, the Kenyan NRF is an independent SGC.

The Kenyan government has a development agenda that focuses on four major areas, namely, food security, health, manufacturing, and housing. The overarching goals to be achieved in these areas are commonly referred to as the "Big Four", and the three institutions of the NSTIC prioritise projects that fall under the Big Four agenda.

With regard to main responsibilities, NACOSTI plays a regulatory role, the NRF deals with facilitation of research, and KeNIA focuses on translation of evidence into practice. NACOSTI plays an oversight role, deciding the research priorities that must be carried out by NRF and KeNIA. NACOSTI sets the research priorities and obtains inputs from wider stakeholders (including the NRF and KeNIA) before the validation of research products for use. KeNIA ensures that research findings are commercialised so as to yield value and support socio-economic development.

The three institutions participate in one another's boards, giving inputs on formulation and implementation processes, and the CEOs have voting rights in all three institutions. Public funds are used for research

FIGURE 3 Organisational structure of the National Research Fund (NRF), Kenya

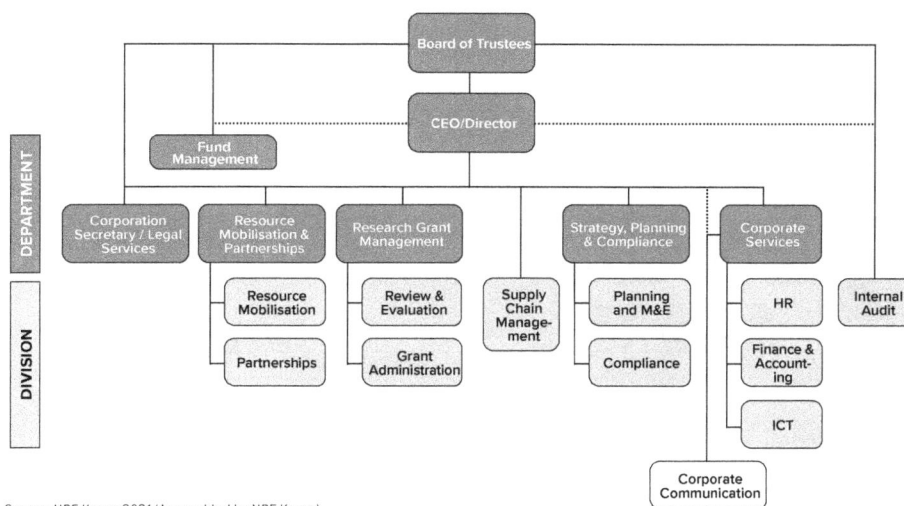

Source: NRF Kenya 2021 (As provided by NRF Kenya)

that falls within national objectives, while funding from other sources can be used for research beyond the national objectives but which must have the potential to contribute to the socio-economic development of the country.

Science granting council in Zambia

The SGC in Zambia is the NSTC, which was established under the Science and Technology Act of 1997. The Council has 13 members drawn from different areas of the science system such as industry, academia, business enterprises, and research institutions. The structure of the NSTC is illustrated in Figure 4. The NSTC is linked to the Ministry of Education, which oversees universities and research institutions, and as such reports to the Minister of Education. At the time that this study was conducted, the portfolio of the Minister for Science and Technology rested within the Ministry of Education.

The Director of Science and Technology, who represents the interest of the Ministry of Education, sits on the NSTC Board. The Board also reports to the Minister. The Board has committees that handle technical issues for the Board – one of which is the Science Technology and Technical Committee. The CEO of the NSTC, who is also the manager responsible

FIGURE 4 Organisational structure of the National Science and Technology Council (NSTC), Zambia

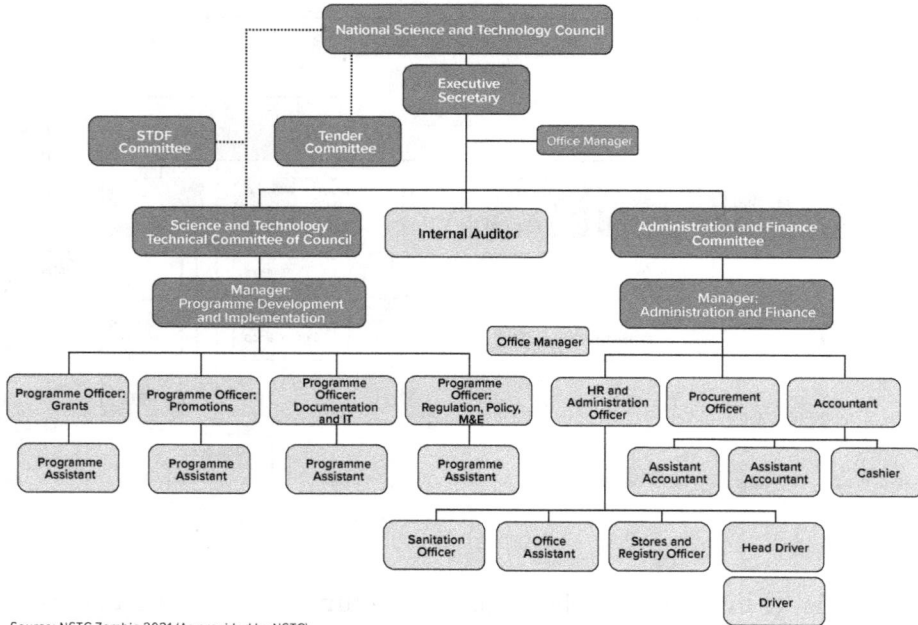

Source: NSTC Zambia 2021 (As provided by NSTC)

for STI activities of the Council, reports to the Science Technology and Technical Committee. Furthermore, the CEO of the Council serves as Secretary of the Council, while another person serves as the Secretary of the Technical Committee. At the time the study was conducted, the NSTC was yet to be constituted by the Minister of Education, who was serving as acting CEO and performing the dual roles of Secretary of the Board and of the Council.

Funding for research

As noted earlier, funding, which is an essential lifeline for research and innovation, is minimal in Africa. The main reason is that there are major competing national needs requiring funding, making it difficult for governments to meet the expectation and commitment to fund R&D at the level of 1% of their GDP. However, some progress has been made towards reaching the target, as illustrated in Table 4. The table compares data on government allocation of GDP to education, higher education, and research during different years (where data are available) for the four African country-cases in this study. These statistics were extracted from the World Bank database,[7,8,9,10] other sources,[11,12,13] and interviews.

TABLE 3 % GDP allocated to different sectors

COUNTRY	EDUCATION (%)	HIGHER EDUCATION AS % OF EDUCATION	RESEARCH (%)
Botswana	9.6% (2009)	42% (2009)	0.54% (2013)
Côte d'Ivoire	5.1% (2017) 15.1 (2020)	14% (2018)	0.09% (2016) 0.37% (2021)
Kenya	5.3% (2015/2017) 19.0% (2018)	13.1% (2015)	0.79% (2010) 0.80% (2021)
Zambia	1.1% (2008) 12.4% (2020)	26% (2005)	0.28% (2008) 0.60% (2021)
South Africa	6.5% (2019) 19.5% (2020)	15% (2018)	0.85% (2022)

Source: Compiled by authors

Table 3 reveals a slight increase over time in the allocation of GDP to research in Zambia, Kenya and Côte d' Ivoire. The SGC in Botswana does not get allocated research funds because their role is mainly coordination and development as well as monitoring and evaluation. Research funds are channeled via different ministries, including the Ministry of Science and Education, which allocates grants to universities and other research entities. "So, we do not have a central research fund like other countries" (Botswana official). Research funding levels in Botswana remain low, with the highest recorded percentage of GDP being 0.5% in 2013. There is great reliance on external funding by higher-education researchers, and such funding is not always aligned to the top priorities of the country or its immediate challenges (Botswana official).

During the interviews, it was mentioned that the NRF in Kenya aims

---

7   https://data.worldbank.org/indicator/SE.XPD.TOTL.GD.ZS?locations=UG&view=chart
8   https://data.worldbank.org/indicator/GB.XPD.RSDV.GD.ZS
9   https://data.worldbank.org/indicator/GB.XPD.RSDV.GD.ZS?locations=ZA
10   https://data.worldbank.org/indicator/SE.XPD.TOTL.GB.ZS?locations=ZG
11   https://www.ceicdata.com/en/kenya/education-statistics/
      ke-government-expenditure-on-education-total--of-gdp
12   https://www.ceicdata.com/en/kenya/technology/
      ke-research-and-development-expenditure--of-gdp
13   https://knoema.com/atlas/Kenya/topics/Education/Expenditures-on-Education/
      Expenditure-in-tertiary-education

to secure adequate funding for research in the country, with the target being to utilise 2% of the GDP to fund research. If Kenya were to reach this target, it would be a good prototype and useful example for other African states. The 2% target for funding in Kenya is expected to be reached with support from other sources such as private sector development partners and philanthropists. From an R&D survey conducted in 2020, 0.8% of the Kenyan GDP (equivalent to approximately USD 80 billion) currently goes to research. Government's contribution since the inception of Kenya's NRF has been between 0.003% and 0.03%; the rest is provided by development partners and the private sector (Kenya official). It is to be noted that in Kenya, while government's revenue was declining due to the negative impact of the pandemic on companies and industries, government still prioritised provision of funds needed for research and to cover the operational costs of the NRF.

Côte d'Ivoire has set its target at 1% of GDP, but currently its research funding level remains at 0.37%. In Zambia, the target is also set at 1%, but research is funded at a lower rate of 0.6% of the GDP. However, the NSTC presents their annual budget to the government at the end of every calendar year and, so far, they have been fortunate enough in some years to get their budget request fully funded. This has been the case in 2017 and 2020. In 2018, they received 75% of their budget request and 80% in 2019. Officials indicated they were grateful that their funding levels never dropped below 70% of their requested budget.

Research links to development agendas

From the literature reviewed, it is evident that research needs to inform policy for the advancement of the development agenda. In the Global North, this seems to be the case more often than in the Global South. However, this study found evidence that this may be changing. A case in point is Botswana, where there is an increase in the number of scholars and academics joining politics (Botswana official). There is an expectation that they will bring their research skills into policy-making processes – a topic worth exploring in greater depth in the future.

In this study, there were many references made to research priorities being informed not only by national development plans but also regional and continental development agendas. For instance, the Steering Committee of PASRES gives direction to the other two units within the organisation (Scientific Council and Executive Secretariat) in terms of priorities at the sub-regional level (e.g., those set by the Economic Community of West African States) as well as national level. For Kenya, the representative in the study said the following: "We are addressing our bigger Vision 2030. We are also addressing the SDGs [Sustainable Development Goals] and of course the African Union Agenda 2063. Our country has a stake in contributing towards continental, and global priorities."

In Zambia, the NSTC developed a five-year strategic plan guided by the 7 National Development Plan (7NPP) and the Vision 2030. "This 7 NPP and Vision 2030 aim to develop a country driven by science, technology, and innovation" (Zambia official). The official further noted that the Council has a responsibility to domesticate the 7NPP and Vision 2030 through the strategic plan. It must also take into consideration the Science and Technology Policy, which was reviewed and relaunched in December 2020. Currently, there is a draft of the national research agenda which clearly indicates all the national priorities in terms of research. According to the same official, the agenda is before the parliament for approval. Once approved, it becomes an official guiding document for different role players in the implementation process.

In the three countries with independent SGCs, there seems to be more coordination in setting research priorities and aligning them to national government agendas. In Côte d'Ivoire, scientific research priorities are set by the Scientific Council. For Kenya, the government has set four major national objectives which frame the research priorities. The National Science, Technology, and Innovation Act 2013 enabled the establishment of agencies that support the pursuit of these priorities. In the case of Zambia, the NSTC sets priorities and outlines them in their five-year strategic plan, which is informed by the government's development agenda. However, in Botswana, in the absence of an independent SGC, different ministries set their own priorities and use their own funds to support research. According to a Botswana official, "when it comes to priorities, to start with, we have a national development plan, so the ministries get their priorities out of the national development plans". The BJC coordinates these various efforts.

Innovation and valorisation of research products for policy impact

Two challenges were identified during the study as barriers to funding research at a higher level. The first is that governments and society at large sometimes do not see the direct value of research. The second issue relates to the continuing tension between using research funds for applied rather than for basic research,[14] as opposed to valuing and supporting both types of research. Funding basic research is perceived as funding academic interests that do not necessarily benefit society. This perception is illustrated by the following statement:

> The only thing that people are doing is that they are researching so they can get promoted but that is not what the government is interested in. We are interested in products and services that can be channelled in the economy to improve the lives of the people. (Botswana official)

This resonates with Chataway et al.'s (2019) study that calls into question knowledge transfer for societal benefit in Africa. With the continent lagging on development indices, there is increased emphasis on directly involving science and technology in pursuit of the innovation required to drive development. Accordingly, the African Union has established the African Union Science, Technology, and Innovation Strategy for Africa (STISA) of 2014. The Strategy sets out a 10-year plan for the continent to mainstream science and technology into plans for Africa to achieve the 2030 UN SDGs (Chataway et al., 2019).

A point that was raised on several occasions by the leadership of the SGCs is that many researchers in academic institutions are only interested in research that would lead to publications and promotion

---

14   "Basic (aka fundamental or pure) research is driven by a scientist's curiosity or interest in a scientific question. The main motivation is to expand man's knowledge, not to create or invent something. There is no obvious commercial value to the discoveries that result from basic research. ... Applied research is designed to solve practical problems of the modern world, rather than to acquire knowledge for knowledge's sake. One might say that the goal of the applied scientist is to improve the human condition" (Lawrence Berkeley National Laboratory, n.d.). https://www.sjsu.edu/people/fred. prochaska/courses/ScWk170/s0/Basic-vs.-Applied-Research.pdf

and not in research that contributes to development in their countries. Uganda's Minister for Science, Technology, and Innovation, Dr Monica Musenero, affirmed this sentiment: "In Africa a lot of us do research with the aim of publishing in academic journals and so as to use such publishing to earn ourselves promotions at work" (Waruru, 2021, 1). Musenero's statement reflects a widely held perception – as evidence by views expressed at high-level fora such as the Seventh African Higher Education Week and the Regional Universities Forum for Capacity Building in Agriculture (RUFORUM) Triennial Conference in 2021. At this conference, some ministers held the view that African scientists only engage in research to produce knowledge with no clear benefit for the larger society. This again underscores "the message to the research community ... that impact-focused research work would compel governments to avail funding, as it would be helping the state make meaningful development strides" (Waruru, 2021, 1).

It thus remains a challenge to persuade governments that contributing to development and producing research that leads to publications are not mutually exclusive. The leadership of the SGCs believe that it is such perceptions that are serving as a barrier to increased research funding. There was also a mentioning of the need to utilise research products to inform policy and an expectation that researchers should make their research accessible by writing policy briefs based on their research. It was noted, however, that not many researchers are producing policy briefs.

Findings from our study show that Kenya and Zambia are intentional in overcoming the challenge of increasing research funding by proactively valorising research outcomes, and other countries are in the process of emulating this. To this end, Kenya National Innovation Agency (KeNIA) has been tasked with valorising research outcomes in Kenya, while the NSTC in Zambia is prioritising identification of impactful research projects to fund. The situation warrants monitoring to learn from their experiences.

An innovative strategy utilised by the NRF in Kenya to create a more positive perception and greater awareness of ongoing research was to produce a documentary on current projects that are in their final stages in order to showcase what has been done so far and to maintain a record of their success. According to an official, this documentary was useful in helping to identify projects that might need to be scaled and financially supported. The CEO further noted that this has proved to be a productive way of presenting what has been achieved through research to the public, relevant authorities, stakeholders and partners for them to see and appreciate what research can contribute in terms of social impact and development.

Botswana is also making important strides in showcasing research results and technological innovations through its National Science Week, which attracts participants from different parts of the world. Furthermore, through the Botswana Innovation Hub, funds have been made available to develop technologies to be applied in dealing with the Covid-19 pandemic. Researchers have, for example, been able to design innovative technologies for registering people for vaccination in easily accessible locations (e.g., parks, shopping centres and places of worship).

Another strategy adopted in Kenya was to identify decision-making bodies responsible for budgetary allocations and engage with them through dialogue. The NRF has directly approached the Parliamentary Committee in charge of education and research, and engaged them in a dialogue that has yielded positive results. In addition, the NRF has developed a resource-mobilisation strategy that is meant to guide the sourcing of research funds available in Kenya. This strategy proposes several models that can be used in raising funds – for instance, a loans scheme providing start-up loans to people who have feasible proposals for business enterprises that would clearly benefit the broader society. An official noted that the NRF should soon move to the implementation phase of this scheme.

Botswana has started targeting some institutions and universities as drivers of innovation with the aim of supporting them as they partner with institutions from other countries. An example is the participation of the Botswana International University of Science and Technology (BIUST) in the Square Kilometre Array (SKA) project – an international partnership led by South Africa and Australia. When completed, the SKA telescope will be the largest of its kind in the world (Teseletso, 2021). A site has been identified at BIUST for the SKA project, and preparations for developments are ongoing. To increase public awareness of such innovative projects, the DRST has launched a radio programme where researchers communicate in an accessible format what they are doing and what they have achieved so far.

Zambia is also proactively working on converting knowledge produced in universities and research centres into tangible products to be utilised for development. A Zambian official had the following to say in this regard:

> Through the funds received from the IDRC in Canada, NSTC has launched a project called Knowledge Translation and Dissemination which aims at packaging all research documents into policy briefs that can be utilised by policy-makers in the areas of industry, gender dynamics, science and technology, development of extra drug resistant treatments to tuberculosis and many more. (Zambia official)

Unfortunately, we were unable to obtain additional information on the valorisation of research products or on strategies utilised to ensure the social impact of research conducted in Côte d'Ivoire.

An innovative strategy that could be explored and utilised by the research community in Africa is to pursue synergistic collaboration amongst African academics on the continent and in the diaspora in order to build a thriving research community that can generate new knowledge relevant to societal transformation. Such wider collaboration is what Ndunda and Maina (2021, 1) refer to as "creating an environment for intellectual capital remittance". An example of an organisation that fosters these international relationships is the Carnegie African Diaspora Fellowship Program (CADFP), which funds African academics to spend time at universities in the US and Canada. The impact of such organisations can have lasting positive effects, with one Carnegie Corporation officer noting that "the CADFP collaborations have sparked innovation, created vibrant research communities, leveraged resources, generated new knowledge and increased research productivity" (University World News, 2021, 1).

Public–private partnerships

The NRF in South Africa has a strategy document for promoting public–private partnerships in research. It has developed the NRF Industry Partnership Strategy (National Research Foundation, 2019), which focuses on supporting and promoting innovative research and human capacity development programmes that involve long-term partnerships between industry and research institutions. This Strategy aims to increase the NRF's responsiveness to industry needs, mobilise resources, and enhance joint programming that promotes social and economic development.

Other SGCs included in the study are also exploring ways to engage the private sector. For example, Botswana is starting to place greater emphasis on the involvement of the private sector in funding research, and they attribute this shift in focus to their participation in the SGCI – particularly the financial support they received during phase one of the SGCI.

> So, we are really thankful to the SGCI because we are working on finalising a strategy aimed at engaging the private sector to participate meaningfully in research. So, that will really help the government … We have also started involving the private sector in activities like our Science Week and the annual researchers' conference. (Botswana official)

There was general acknowledgement that research activities carried out by the private sector and non-government agencies are likely to benefit the broader society, and a partnership with them will contribute to addressing national needs. One challenge raised was that "the private sector and industry in Botswana are predominantly subsidiaries of entities elsewhere, so research and development for those entities are done elsewhere, and only what is deployed here are the services and the products that come out of that and the work" (Botswana official).

It was again mentioned that diaspora researchers should be encouraged to participate in research that would benefit the country. This is an idea that needs to be explored further, as there are initiatives – mainly in the economic sector – that encourage the diaspora to contribute to development projects in Africa. An example of this is the African Diaspora Network, which raises capital from the African diaspora and friends of Africa to support development efforts. In the education sphere, the previously mentioned CADFP has awarded well over 500 fellowships to scholars from more than 160 universities in Africa to support research, curriculum development, and teaching activities (University World News, 2021).

In Kenya, strong public–private partnerships also exist, with the NRF providing funding for researchers in the private sector as well as academia. The private sector is represented on the NRF board, but there are still challenges in achieving more active participation from the private sector. Research focused on the Big Four priority areas (food security, universal health coverage, manufacturing, and housing) is often supported through public funds, while research in other areas generally has to rely on privately raised funds.

Another form of partnership that was highlighted by study participants is the partnership between SGCs in different countries. Examples include the partnership between Botswana and Zimbabwe, which has led to joint calls for research funded through the IDRC, as well as calls made by the South African NRF, which is leveraging funding from external funding agencies to support researchers in Botswana. It is to be noted that for the partnership between Botswana and Zimbabwe, each country is contributing 15% to the research project funds. Currently, two research projects are ongoing, with the Principal Investigators coming from Botswana and Zimbabwe. The Botswana Innovation Hub and the Research Council of Zimbabwe are collaborating to manage the projects. In addition, there are plans to create a research monitoring system that is externally funded and includes a database of research being conducted as well as mechanisms that would allow for the sharing of equipment. Progress has been made in setting up this system, but at the time the study interviews were conducted, there were delays due to technical challenges faced by the DSRT. However, the Department envisages that the system will be complete by March 2022.

In Zambia, the SGC partners with the private sector by organising joint activities. According to an official,

> Yearly, the Zambian Science Conference is organised and a central theme jointly developed with its partners. This initiative, which started in 2016, targets a particular industry every year, such as the agro-processing, livestock, etc. (Zambia official)

This is their strategy to network and connect a wide range of industries under a single canopy. Another partner to the NSTC is the Zambian Association of Manufacturers (ZAAM). According to a Zambia official, this is an institution that focuses more on manufacturers, and it is in the interest of the Council to partner with them in order to, first, collect information on investment by private sector in their own research to generate value-added products and, second, to utilise ZAAM to attract other industries to fund research. The Council is in the process of signing a memorandum of understanding with ZAAM.

The NSTC also strives to play the role of a facilitator by creating linkages between the industries, the knowledge generators, and the universities. The goal is to narrow the interaction gap amongst stakeholders that might negatively impact research outputs and limit the social impact of research. A Zambia official noted that, in the quest to motivate industries to participate in partnerships with the NSTC, the Council plans to collect data on the industries' in-house investment in R&D. The goal is to find measures to introduce tax incentives for companies. The Act establishing the Council empowers it to make a case to government to give tax rebates to companies investing in research. The aim is to involve the private sector more and to promote partnerships with them.

The situation in Côte d'Ivoire is similar. Based on the information collected, partnerships with the private sector exist and are valued. According to an official, "the private sector is seen as a close partner because the country's economy depends on the sector, whose engagement is majorly in agriculture". This is why PASRES is actively pursuing involvement by the private sector in order to maximise the benefits of these relationships and thereby expand the support base for research in Côte d'Ivoire.

Unlocking research funds

Aside from valorising research outcomes, there are other strategies being developed to unlock more research funds from a variety of sources. For example, Botswana is considering expanding its RSTI space by attracting more partners to join and participate in research. According to a Botswana official, "in addition to funding, what I think is very critical is for us to grow our RSTI landscape ... I believe once we get that, every other thing, including funding, will fall in the right direction."

The other strategy mentioned is that of bringing policy-makers into a dialogue on the benefits of research and how research products could be used to benefit society. A Botswana official noted that research is an investment that may yield visible result within a short or longer period, and that the results might be usable immediately or not. The official argued that this understanding is needed on the part of policy-makers and can be achieved through open dialogue.

As noted in the preceding section, government incentives to the private sector would go a long way in unlocking more funds for research and innovation. As is the practice in South Africa, where incentives are given in the form of tax breaks, Zambia and Kenya are in the process of adopting the same strategy. According to a Zambia official,

> in the quest to motivating the industries, the Council is trying to collect their in-house investment on R&D. Given that the Act empowers the Council to initiate tax incentives, the Council can make a case for them before the government to give tax rebate. This is a move to draw the industries close and for them to open up more on what is it that they do. (Zambia official)

A Kenyan official noted that "an area where the NRF needs some assistance would be the area of resource mobilisation from the private sector. Soft skills are needed in this area to be able to approach them the best way."

PASRES, which understands the role of the private sector and has an established partnership with the private sector since 2007, has not been able to consolidate that relationship. They hope to improve on this by learning from what other SGCs are doing. One official noted:

> The private sector is key in that many governments in Africa cannot adequately provide the scientific research and innovation needs thus the need for partnership with them. This is why Côte d'Ivoire takes the private sector very important for the mobilisation of funding for scientific research in the country. (Côte d'Ivoire official)

On the other side, the research community has been advised that a change in research focus would not only produce knowledge that would benefit the society but would motivate governments to make funding available for research (Waruru, 2021). Taking the argument further, Uganda's Minister for Science, Technology, and Innovation, Dr Monica Musenero, noted that:

> we need to challenge our academia to change their research models and start doing research that ends in a product out there in the market, or a business start-up. That is what happens in many countries that have relied on knowledge production to achieve development. (Waruru, 2021, 1)

The preceding indicates that, aside from pursuing partnerships with the private sector, the research community should look inwards and explore ways to garner additional government support.

In the following section, we discuss issues that emerged during the study that were not anticipated or included in the original study design.

Emergent issues

Equity and diversity

The concepts of equity and diversity were not originally included as part of the study; however, these issues emerged in some of the discussions with the participants. All the sampled SGCs take the issue of equity and diversity seriously, yet none of the SGCs has a specific equity and diversity policy.

Equity and diversity reflect skeletally in some of the official documents and are to varying degrees taken into consideration in the allocation of funding to researchers. A case in point is Botswana. In discussions with an official, it was mentioned that their research policy specifically supports women researchers. For example, there has been a strong focus on ensuring women get their PhDs. In one of the Botswana DRST training projects, women constituted 70% of participants. In addition, their projects target high school students to raise awareness of and promote science and technology career options; the goal is for participants to be represented in a ratio of three girls to one boy.

Although SGC officials mentioned that they allocate funds with sensitivity to gender equity, it is important for SGCs to develop clear policy documents to describe policies related to equity and diversity and related implementation strategies.

Impact of Covid-19: Challenges, prioritisation, and lessons learned

Globally, Covid-19 has changed the way individuals and organisations go about their daily activities. SGCs are no exception, and they have been affected in different ways. Many countries were forced into lockdown and implemented various other efforts with far-reaching impacts. As restrictions have eased, the world has had to adapt to what is widely termed "the new normal". This section covers the challenges, changes in prioritisation, and lesson learned by SGCs during the pandemic that emerged during the study interviews.

Due to a lack of infrastructure enabling them to effectively operate remotely, many SGCs were impacted negatively by the restrictions associated with the Covid-19 pandemic. It was reported that some of the officials and researchers had difficulties working from home, as they faced challenges such as inadequate connectivity and power outages. Consequently, in some instances, SGC officials had to take turns working at their offices, which slowed operations down substantially. This was the case for all the four SGCs sampled for this study.

There were also challenges relating to the acquisition of the needed equipment, such as modems, which were not budgeted for, and some-times received push-back from finance departments or treasuries due to strict spending regulations. There were also costs related to home or mobile phone usage by officials – especially those charged with responsibilities to monitor and evaluate research. Special applications had to be made to allow funds to be used for those purposes.

In addition to technological challenges, it was mentioned that at times, there was a slow-down in decision making processes and in day-to-day operations due to staff being in isolation or quarantine.

The Covid-19 pandemic forced countries to revisit their research priorities and restructure their budgets to address emergent challenges. As mentioned by the Botswana representative:

> There have been budget cuts in the original budgets that were allocated to some of the research organisations, which is quite disabling, because if we are having a [inaudible] like this and all, then we are taking from the researchers. How are you going to solve the problem? Yeah, so it is the problem that we are facing.

This revision of priorities and funding allocation is not peculiar to the sampled countries alone. South Africa, which is seen as a model by some of the SGCs, was significantly affected as well – particularly when the Minister of Higher Education, Science, and Innovation announced cuts to its science and innovation budget as the country adjusted its spending priorities to focus on the containment of Covid-19 (Space in Africa, 2020). This led to the launch of different programmes by the NRF aimed at mobilising and supporting the scientific community to find local solutions to mitigate the impact of the pandemic.

The Botswana Innovation Hub allocated funds through the Botswana Innovation Fund for Covid-19-related projects. The positive outcome of this is that, in a short period of time, different technologies were developed for use in the management of the Covid-19 pandemic. Botswana also reported the emergence of various new local technologies. An example is the development of applications that assisted in registration for vaccinations in the shopping centres, religious centres, and buses. There were also tools developed for easy contact tracing. Thus, while Covid-19 had its negative effects, it also spurred nations such as Botswana to develop their own technologies to address challenges. Many of these local technologies will remain useful post-Covid-19.

In Côte d'Ivoire, where government prioritises research that impacts lives positively, the Minister for Higher Education Scientific Research approved the mobilisation of the scientific community to assist the government at the start of the Covid-19 pandemic in March 2020. The aim was to put local knowledge to use to identify the Covid-19 virus strain that first entered the country in an attempt to find local solutions to curb or cure the virus. It was also important to know how to communicate effectively to the public regarding safety measures such as social distancing, given that Africans generally tend to live a more communal lifestyle. Solutions from the Global North involved mitigation measures that included isolation if symptomatic and avoidance of social gatherings to prevent spread of the virus. According to a Côte d'Ivoire official, these practices are contrary to social norms in African cultures, where family and friends tend to gather together to support the ill or bereaved. Communicating and motivating the public to follow recommended safety measures was thus a big challenge for the health sector in Côte d'Ivoire which needed urgent solutions. Half of PASRES' funds were re-allocated to launch a special call in that regard. In addition to this, more funding was received after strategic lobbying by the Executive Secretary. The research community responded positively and proposed workable solutions to address the challenges faced by the health sector. According to a representative:

> This project was a huge success as scientists from the health sciences were mobilised to carryout scientific study, and researchers from the social science and humanities were also mobilised to address how to effectively communicate to the people in the light of long-existed cultural values which negates what the situation demands from the people were mobilised. (Côte d'Ivoire official)

The implementation of these solutions has, according to the SGC, yielded impressive results thus far.

The NRF in Kenya launched strategic calls for research on Covid-19 as well as two other major areas of concern – namely, cancer and locust invasion. The calls were processed and, due to financial constraints, funding was allocated on a priority basis. According to a Kenya official, resources were allocated to a consortium to address Covid-19 research in four thematic areas: (i) biotechnology research and clinical trials as well as drug development and trials, (ii) psychosocial health, (iii) public health, and (iv) Covid-19 prevention.

It was also reported that newly identified research areas linked to the Big Four priorities before the Covid-19 pandemic were paused so that research on the Covid-19-related challenges could be funded, and research funds were re-allocated accordingly. There are many new information and communication technology interventions/solutions related to Covid-19 challenges documented. These include, amongst other interventions, the automation of various processes which were previously implemented manually.

Unlike Côte d'Ivoire, where additional funds were allocated, no additional funding was initially allocated in Kenya, but priorities were re-organised. However, after negotiations with the relevant authorities, the NRF anticipates that additional funding will be made available as budgets are reviewed and adjusted to address urgent priorities. Specific dates for these review processes were not provided. Covid-19 has interrupted many programmes and ongoing research projects. The organisation is yet to get actual reports on which programmes were affected in Kenya. However, the NRF aims to use this report as a basis for promoting policy that would recognise researchers as essential workers. The pandemic has exposed this lacuna and revealed the need to add researchers to the list of essential workers when there is a public health crisis of this nature.

Zambia's NSTC also launched an emergency call for Covid-19-related research in 2020. We were unable to find more information as to progress made in this regard.

Overall, the interviewees confirmed that there were various positive outcomes as countries were pushed to develop technological solutions to the challenges posed by Covid-19.

One common feature that emerged from the study discussions related to the Covid-19 pandemic is the emergence of interventions and lessons that have permanently changed the SGCs' modes of operation moving forward.

The first lesson learned during the crisis was that where governments saw immediate impact of research to society as was the case with Covid-19 period, they were willing to put more money or redirect funds for such research activities. From the case studies, governments swiftly made funding available for research that aimed to make use of indigenous knowledge system to further generate knowledge that would help the citizens cope during the Covid-19 period and survive the Covid-19 virus.

The second lesson points to the fact that these institutions (SGCs) can continue to operate with fewer personnel, as long as they have the technological infrastructure. A case in point is Botswana, where the DRST had been contemplating operating with a leaner structure. The Department is currently working towards relying more on technology support for operations than having many people operate a manual system. The plan is to learn from peers such as the NRF South Africa, the African Academy of Sciences, and global networks of evaluators and experts to establish a system of experts who will evaluate proposals when calls are put out.

The third lesson relates to the importance of investing in technological infrastructure –particularly online connectivity – for dealing with future crises and particularly to more effectively support remote operation. Botswana is making significant progress in this regard. The Ministry of Tertiary Education, Research, Science, and Technology, through the DRST, has initiated a research management system. The intention is to collect and safely store data on research activities and outcomes so that there is continuous monitoring of activities in the research community, the sharing of equipment, funding allocations, research outputs, and various other information that is needed. This system is in the final stages of development.

The fourth lesson is the benefit of an automated system. If there is an effective system in place, the SGC can operate more effectively. After setting up a more advanced system in Zambia, there was more efficiency in the disbursement of funds. In addition, the NSTC had an increased inflow of grants from various partners and donors. For example, the Council got funding from IDRC for tri-lateral and bi-lateral calls. Universities also improved their systems and replaced the use of a centralised account for fund disbursement with special accounts opened for specific projects to facilitate simpler project implementation.

5

Towards a Formidable Research and Innovation Base

for Sustainable Development in Africa

Our findings have touched on several pertinent issues relateds to the governance and funding of the SGCs in Africa. There are findings that have strong links to the effective management and functioning of the SGCs. For clarity, we provide a summary of each finding below.

Management of the science granting councils

The human resources of the SGCs vary. According to the interviews conducted, Kenya operates on lean but efficient human capacity, with the NRF having only three technical officers. In Zambia, there were only 13 NSTC personnel, while the number of PASRES staff in in Côte d'Ivoire could not be determined. Interestingly, in Botswana – the only country in the study without an independent SGC – the DRST seemed to require far greater human resource capacity to manage, with 33 staff members (core and support/admin staff). We recommend that governments work towards establishing independent SGCs that operate with lean structures to save resources that can be used to fund research activities. This is one way to reduce the cost of running these institutions and make more funds available for research purposes.

Funding of research

A major problem identified in the funding of research is that most politicians expect research products to be tangible and immediately usable for them to justify the funding of research. This is a real challenge, because the path from inception to products and services is not a smooth and linear one. To address this issue, it is important for SGCs and other agencies to find mechanisms to valorise and commercialise research products. In the case of Kenya, an agency such as KeNIA has been charged with this responsibility.

The points raised in the following section on linking research to development agendas are also potential ways of unlocking more research funds.

Research links to development agendas

There is evidence that research priorities in the case study countries are aligned to national development agendas; however, there is no evidence that the research outputs are used to advance the development agenda. To address this issue, we make three recommendations. The first is that deliberate efforts be made to ensure that research outputs reach end users – for example, farmers producing food. The second recommendation is that SGCs encourage researchers to co-generate knowledge with communities by forming partnerships with community organisations in the field that their research targets. The third is to deliberately prioritise and pursue the informing of policy by research. This can be achieved through SGCs organising policy dialogues and engagements between policy-makers, researchers and the broader community. Such dialogues will create a platform for making research outcomes more accessible and usable than if they are only disseminated through scholarly publications and papers presented at conferences. However, it must be acknowledged that implementing these recommendations requires additional financial and human resources.

The four frames of action proposed by St John (2013) and discussed in chapter 2 provides a useful framework on how best to structure and utilise both qualitative and quantitative research to inform policy. With reference to the above recommendations, we particularly advise the use of the communicative frame, whereby government agencies and researchers collaborate with one another to find new ways to address challenges.

Innovation and valorisation of research products for policy impact

The potential beneficial impact of research on a society cannot be over emphasised. As it has been noted earlier in the report, research products should be key drivers in policy-making processes in order to support societal development. Accordingly, SGCs need to continuously find innovative ways in which knowledge produced can be maximally utilised for the benefit of the people. The creation of the SGCI has been one significant development in advancing cooperation amongst SGCs so that they can more effectively share information and learn from one another. Furthermore, initiatives that support collaboration amongst African academics – both continent-wide and internationally – can be tremendously impactful in promoting better research with greater potential for impact on the African continent.

Public–private partnerships

An important strategy that could be adopted by SGCs to encourage partnerships with the private sector is to offer incentives such as tax rebates. The SGCs in Kenya and Zambia are planning to utilise an approach in line with the system that operates in South Africa. The South African government offers an R&D incentive, which was introduced into the Income Tax Act in 2006. Section 11D of the Act allows for a deduction equal to 150% of expenditure incurred directly for R&D. This incentive is designed to further encourage industry to undertake R&D (National Rresearch Foundation, 2019). This offers a model for others to follow.

Unlocking research funds

As it has been established, the private sector remains a key stakeholder vis-à-vis research and innovation. Therefore, if appealing incentives for funding research are introduced, there is a greater likelihood that the private sector would be willing to invest in R&D. However, caution should be exercised in ensuring that development agenda priorities are not redefined and skewed in the interests of investors only. In addition, a continued dialogue with policy-makers is essential to get the support needed for the funding of research.

* * *

Further general recommendations are made based on two main data sources: issues that emerged in the literature review and the study findings from interactions with the SGCI community.

First, our findings from both data sources show that the SGCI in Africa has proven to be an important and viable initiative, as SGCs play a pivotal role in attracting more funding for R&D in Africa. It is thus important that this initiative be strengthened and efforts consolidated so that R&D in Africa can attract the necessary funding.

Second, our findings from the literature show that valorisation of research product is still lacking in Africa due to a combination of factors related to researchers and policy-makers; these factors have been explicitly discussed above. We suggest that in order for valorisation of research to be effectively achieved, policy briefs should be made a part of the expected outcomes of funded research. This would partly address the issue of linking research to policy in Africa.

Third, the frames of action proposed by St John (2013) offer different modes of linking researchers with policy-makers and how they interact with each other in the process of carrying out research for policy impact. We recommend utilising the two modes which encourage and facilitate a healthy interaction between policy-makers and researchers. The first is the instrumental frame, which allows policy-makers to commission evaluative studies that would assess the effectiveness of their policies. Second is the open-strategic frame, where researchers focus on the production of information and new ideas that policy-makers could use to address current policy challenges. To implement these ideas, special grants could be made available to address the production of timely knowledge to inform policies in the pipeline or practices in a specific context. In addition, general grants can still be provided for other research projects with more long-term benefits.

Fourth, funding levels for research in all African states remain below 1% of GDP. However, some progress has been made by various governments in increasing their funding levels. This is an area where the good work needs to be continued in advocating for additional resources and to obtain funding allocation for R&D of at least 1% of GDP.

Fifth, there are innovations and models which are unique to individual SGCs in terms of improving their governance structures, valorising research, and mobilising all concerned stakeholders within and beyond national borders. In the three case study countries with independent SGCs, there seems to be more coordination in setting research priorities and aligning them to national government agendas. These individual models could be explored by other SGCs for the purpose of improving and consolidating their governance structures and boosting their funding capacity for the benefit of the research communities in various countries. These efforts will ultimately achieve the goal of improving the lives of the end users of the research products.

It is important for the research community to take seriously research for knowledge production, as well as to ensure that their research products can inform policy for the betterment of the general well-being of the citizenry where possible. This plays an important role in attracting more funding from both the private sector and government for research across Africa.

This study further corroborates existing literature vis-à-vis funding of research in Africa. A major problem identified is that most politicians expect research products to be tangible and usable for them to justify the funding of research. Currently, there is a lack of sufficient research outputs of this kind on the one hand, and a lack of awareness of what is being achieved and produced by research on the other hand. Both issues need to be addressed by SGCs.

In addition, it is also important for SGCs in Africa to cooperate and stay abreast of one another's operations to learn from one another and establish best practices. This approach would enable SGCs to grow and improve within the shortest possible period. For instance, NRF Kenya has indicated the need for some assistance in soft skills needed for resource mobilisation from the private sector. An innovative strategy followed by the NRF Kenya was to create a documentary on current research projects that have been in progress for several years and are in their final stages. This documentary showcased the achievements and successes of these projects to a broad public audience – an example of an approach that could be explored by other SGCs.

African countries need research that not only produces useful products but that can effectively inform policy for research to have the maximum social impact and contribute to development on the continent. Innovative strategies are needed to achieve this – one of which is partnering with African academics in the diaspora for research collaborations that can yield the products needed for Africa's transformation and development. Furthermore, researchers should be encouraged to make their research more accessible and visible. If policy-makers see the direct benefit, they are more likely to make additional funds available.

An area for further research that emerged prominently from this study is exploring how to effectively use research for greater societal impact and not only for academic advancement.

References

Adekanmbi, G., Kasozi, J. A., Seabelo, C. and Batisani, C. 2021. Pre-and Post-COVID-19: Exploring Issues of Access in Higher Education in Botswana and Ghana. *Alliance for African Partnership Perspectives*, 1(1), 125–135

Adelowo M. C., Akinwale. O. Y. and Olaopa R. O. 2017. Innovation and Knowledge Transfer in Nigeria. *International Journal of Research Innovation and Commercialisation*, 1(1), 57–73

Adjei, F. and Nintin, R. 2018. A Baseline Assessment of Public-Private Partnerships in Research and Scientific Cooperation in Ivory Coast. *SGCI in Sub-Saharan Africa – Strengthening Partnerships among Africa's Science Granting Councils and the Private Sector*

African Academy of Sciences (AAS). 2017. Harnessing Botswana's Development Success to Promote Science, Technology and Innovation. *AAS Country Profile 2017.*

African Economic Outlook. 2012. *Zambia 2012.* AfdB, OECD, UNDP, UNECA

African Technology Policy Studies Network (ATPS). 2020. Networking Africa's Science Granting Councils: Building Partnerships and Networks among Science Granting Councils and Other Science Actors in Sub-Saharan Africa, *Final Technical Report.* IDRC

African Union Development Agency-NEPAD (AUDA-NEPAD). 2017. *About us.* https://www.nepad.org/who-we-are/about-us

Agency for the Promotion of European Research (APRE). 2015. The South African Innovation Landscape and Framework Conditions to Support Collaboration between South Africa and the European Union. *APRE Working Papers* 3.1 & 3.2

Ajulor, O. V. 2018. The Challenges of Policy Implementation in Africa and Sustainable Development Goals. *PEOPLE: International Journal of Social Sciences,* 3(3), 1497–1518

Archer, S. 2017. The Function of a University in South Africa: Part 1. *South African Journal of Science,* 113(5/6), 1–6

Ariail, D. L. 2016. Globalisation of Higher Education in South Africa. *Georgia Journal of College Student Affairs,* 32, 30–35

Arvanitis, R. and Mouton, J. 2019. Observing and Funding African Research. *CEPED Working Paper* 43, September. DOI: 10.5281/zenodo.3403895

Awuor, E. 2013. The African Knowledge Transfer Partnership (AKTP): Challenges and Achievements. *Journal of Economics and Sustainable Development,* 4(5), 1–5

Ayisi, J., Ndakala, F., Nyanga, R., Daniels, C., Owuor, R., Ting, B. and Wanyaman, B. 2019. Assessing the Potential for Transformative Innovation Policy in Kenya. *Transformative Innovation Policy: Africa Hub,* March

Badat, S. and Prozesky, W. 1994. *Science Councils: Towards the Democratisation of Governance (Report for the Science and Technology Initiative).* Mimeo.

Baliyan, S. P. and Moorad, F. R. 2018. Teaching Effectiveness in Private Higher Education Institutions in Botswana: Analysis of Students' Perceptions. *International Journal of Higher Education,* 7(8), 143–155

Bailey, T. 2010. The Research–Policy Nexus: Mapping the Terrain of the Literature. Paper prepared for the Higher Education Research and Advocacy Network in Africa (HERANA). Centre for Higher Education Transformation (CHET)

Bailey, T. 2015. The Role of National Councils and Commissions in African Higher Education System Governance. In Cloete, N., Maassen, P. and Bailey, T. (Eds), *Knowledge Production and Contradictory Functions in African Higher Education* (171–202). African Minds. https://doi.org/10.5281/zenodo.824881

Berg, S. V. and Hofmeyr, H. (2018). *Education in South Africa. World Bank Republic of South Africa Systematic Country Diagnostic, An Incomplete Transition: Overcoming the Legacy of Exclusion in South Africa.* The World Bank.

Bertelsmann Stiftung Index (BTI). 2022. *BTI Country Report: South Africa.* Bertelsmann Stiftung

Bertelsmann Stiftung. 2020. *Bertelsmann Stiftung's Transformation Index (BTI) 2020 Country Report: Zambia.* Bertelsmann Stiftung

Boit, J. M. and Kipkoech, L. C. 2012. Liberalization of Higher Education in Kenya: Challenges and Prospects. *International Journal of Academic Research in Progressive Education and Development,* 1(2), 44–53

Bolo, M. O. 2020. *Developing a Social and Behaviour Change (SBC) and Advocacy Strategy for Science Granting Councils in Sub-Saharan Africa: A Localization Guide.* Strategy for Science Granting Councils

Botswana Hub. 2022. List of Universities & Colleges in Botswana. http://www.botswanahub.com/list-of-universities-colleges-in-botswana/

The Botswana Gazette. 2021. Botswana's 2021/22 Budget Breakdown. *The Gazette.* https://www.thegazette.news/business/botswanas-2021-22-budget-breakdown/

Broadbent, E. 2012. *Politics of Research-based Evidence in African Policy Debates: Synthesis of Case Study Findings*. Evidence Based Policy in Development Network (EBPDN). https://www.alnap.org/system/files/content/resource/files/main/126565-ebpdn-synthesis-1.pdf

Bunting, I., Cloete, N., Wah, H. L. K. and Nakayiwa-Mayega, F. 2015. Assessing the Performance of African Flagship Universities. In Cloete, N., Maassen, P. and Bailey, T. (Eds), *Knowledge Production and Contradictory Functions in African Higher Education* (32–60). African Minds. https://doi.org/10.5281/zenodo.824654

Centre for Higher Education Transformation (CHET). 2017. Bibliometric Report on Herana Universities. Prepared by DST-NRF Centre for Excellence in Scientometrics and Science Technology and Policy, Stellenbosch University

Chataway, J., Dobson, C., Daniels, C., Byrne, R., Hanlin, R. and Tigabu, A. 2019. Science Granting Councils in Africa: Trends and Tensions. *Science and Public Policy*, 46(4), 620–631. DOI: 10.1093/scipol/scz007

Chataway, J., Ochieng, C., Byrne, R., Daniels, C., Dobson, C., Hanlin, R., Hopkins, M. and Tigabu, A. 2017. Case Studies of the Political Economy of Science Granting Councils in Sub-Saharan Africa. *Full Report to the International Development Research Centre, Science Policy Research Unit, University of Sussex, United Kingdom and African Centre for Technology Studies*

Chikalipah, S. and Makina, D. 2019. Economic Growth and Human Development: Evidence from Zambia. *Sustainable Development*, 27, 1023-1033. DOI: 10.1002/sd.1953

Cloete, N. and Maasen, P. 2015. Roles of Universities and the African Context. In Cloete, N., Maassen, P. and Bailey, T. (Eds), *Knowledge Production and Contradictory Functions in African Higher Education* (1–17). African Minds. https://doi.org/10.5281/zenodo.824648

Cloete, N., Bailey, T. and Maassen, P. 2011. *Universities and Economic Development in Africa: Pact, Academic Core and Coordination: Executive Summary of Synthesis Report*. CHET

Cloete, N., Bunting, I. and Maassen, P. 2015. Research Universities in Africa: An Empirical Overview of Eight Flagship Universities. In Cloete, N., Maassen, P. and Bailey, T. (Eds), *Knowledge Production and Contradictory Functions in African Higher Education* (18–31). African Minds. https://doi.org/10.5281/zenodo.824652

Cloete, N., Bunting, I. and Van Schalkwyk, F. 2018. *Research Universities in Africa*. African Minds. https://doi.org/10.47622/9781928331872

Cloete, N., Maassen, P., Bunting, I., Bailey, T., Wangenge-Ouma, G. and Van Schalkwyk, F. 2015. Managing Contradictory Functions and Related Policies Issues. In Cloete, N., Maassen, P. and Bailey, T. (Eds), *Knowledge Production and Contradictory Functions in African Higher Education* (260–289). African Minds. https://doi.org/10.5281/zenodo.824891

De Beers Group. 2021. Our Contribution. https://www.debeersgroup.com/sustainability/our-contribution

Department for Business, Energy and Industrial Strategy. 2022. *Partner Country Case Study: South Africa: Final Evaluation of the Newton Fund*. The National Archives

Department of Higher Education and Training (DHET). 2021. *Report on the Evaluation of the 2019 Universities' Research Output*. DHET

Department of Higher Education and Training (DHET). 2023. *Statistics on Post-School Education and Training in South Africa: 2021*. DHET.

Depatment of Science and Innovation (DSI). 2022. *Innovation Decadal Plan: An instrument for enabling Africa's Reawakening and Inclusive and Sustainable Development*. DSI

Department of Science and Technology (DST). 2018. Draft White Paper on Science, Technology and Innovation. *Government Gazette* No. 41909. Government Printer

DiJohn, J. 2010. State Resilience against the Odds: An Analytical Narrative on the Construction and Maintenance of Political Order in Zambia since 1960. *Crisis States Research Centre Working Papers* No. 75 (June)

Diyamett, B., Makundi, H. and Sheikheldin, G. 2019. Science, Technology and Innovation (STI) Policy Training for Africa: A Basic Module on Reconciling Theory, Practice and Policies. *A Handbook Prepared by STIPRO on behalf of the ACTS Consortium under the Science Granting Councils' Initiative (SGCIs) Theme III*

Dosso, M., Kleibrink, A. and Matusiak, M. 2020. Smart Specialisation Strategies in sub-Saharan Africa: Opportunities, Challenges and Initial Mapping for Cote d'Ivoire. *African Journal of Science, Technology, Innovation and Development*, 1–14. DOI:10.1080/20421338.2020.1816265

Edinger, H. and Mackenzie, B. 2016. *Kenya: Grounding Africa's Economic Growth*. Deloitte

Fedderke, J. W., Lourenco, F. and Gwenhamo, F. 2011. Alternative Indices of Political Freedoms, Property Rights and Political Instability for Zambia. *Working Paper* No. 207 (March)

Ferreira, J. J. and Carayannis, E. G. 2019. University–Industry Knowledge Transfer: Unpacking the 'Black Box'. *Knowledge Management Research & Practice*, 17(4), 353–357

Fillippetti, A. and Savonna, M. 2017. University-Industry Linkages and Academic Engagements: Individual Behaviours and Firms' Barriers. *Journal of Technology Transfer*, 42, 719–729

Forson, J. A. 2017. Innovation Financing and Public Policy Dilemmas in the Economic Community of West African States (ECOWAS), *MPRA Paper* No. 102432 (December)

Fosci, M. and Loffreda, L. 2019. *Strengthening Research Institutions in Africa: A Synthesis Report*. DFID

Fosci, M., Loffreda, L., Chamberlain, A. and Naidoo, N. 2019. *Assessing the Needs of the Research System in Kenya. Report for the SRIA Programme*. DFID

Gaillard, J. and Van Lill, M. 2014. *Science Granting Councils in Sub-Saharan Africa. Country Report: Côte d'Ivoire*. Centre for Research on Evaluation, Science and Technology (CREST), Stellenbosch University

Gluckman, P. 2013. *The Role of Evidence in Policy Formation and Implementation: A Report from the Prime Minister's Chief Science Advisor*. New Zealand: Office of Prime Minister's Science Advisory Committee

Gore, O. T. and Walker, M. 2020. Conceptualising (Dis)advantage in South African Higher Education: A Capability Approach Perspective. *Critical Studies in Thinking and Learning*, 8(2) 55–73

Haas, B. and Kwaak, V. 2017. Exploring Linkages between Research, Policy and Practice in the Netherlands: Perspectives on Sexual and Reproductive Health and Rights Knowledge Flows. *Research Policy and Systems*, 15(40), 1–13

Habermas, J. 1987. *The Theory of Communicative Action: Vol. 2. Lifeworld and System: A Critique of Functionalist Reasoning* (T. McCarthy, trans.). Beacon

Hanlin, R., and Tigabu, A. 2017. *Case Studies of the Political Economy of Science Granting Councils in Sub-Saharan Africa*. IDRC, SPRU and ACTS

Hanlin, R., Numi, A., Daniels, C., Byrne, R. and Pointel, S. 2020. *Updating the Case Studies of the Political Economy of Science Granting Councils in Sub-Saharan Africa: National Case Study of Tanzania*. IDRC, SPRU and ACTS

Harris, R. 2015. The Impact of Research on Development Policy and Practice: This Much We Know. In Chib, A., May, J. and Barrantes, R. (Eds), *Impact of Information Society Research in the Global South* (21–43). Springer

Higher Education Authority (HEA). 2021. *The State of Higher Education in Zambia 2020: Teaching and Learning in the New Normal*. HEA.

Iizuka, M., Konté, A., Mawoko, P., Calza, E. and Gault, F. 2018. Innovation for Development in West Africa: Challenges for Promoting ST&I Policy. *United Nations University Policy Brief* (November)

International Monetary Fund (IMF). 2016. Côte d'Ivoire: Economic Development Documents – National Development Plan, 2016-2020. *IMF Country Report* No. 16/388 (December)

Isaacs, N., Middleton, L., Lynch, I., Essop, R., Fluks, L., Marinda, E., Magampa, M., Majokweni, P., Agugua, A., Kuetche, I., Djoukouo, F., Ndina, C. and Van Rooyen, H. 2021. Strengthening Gender Inclusivity in the National System of Science Technology and Innovation (STI). *Botswana Country Profile, Science Granting Council Initiative, Strengthening the Capacities of Science Granting Councils in Gender and Inclusivity, Human Sciences Research Council*

Ivorian Center for Economic and Social Research (CIRES). 2016. Evaluation of the Environment of Research in Social Sciences: The Case of the Ivory Coast. *Doing Research in Social Sciences Final Draft Report* (April)

Jacobs, P. T., Habiyaremye, A., Fakudze, B., Ramoroka, K. and Jonas, S. 2019. Producing Knowledge to Raise Rural Living Standards: How Universities Connect with Resource-poor Municipalities in South Africa. *The European Journal of Development Research*, 31, 881–901

Jauhiainen, J. S. and Hooli, L. 2017. Indigenous Knowledge and Developing Countries' Innovation Systems: The Case of Namibia. *International Journal of Innovation Studies*, 1(1), 89–106

Jaumont, F. 2016. *Unequal Partners*. Palgrave Macmillan

Kasimba, P. M. 2020. Quality Assurance in Zambian Higher Education: A New Dawn. *International Journal of Science and Research*, 9(5), 930–934

Kauffeldt, J. K. 2009. The Commission for Higher Education in Kenya: A Case Study regarding the Establishment, Role and Operations of an Intermediary Body in the Higher Education System of a Developing Nation. PhD Dissertation, Ontario Institute for Studies in Education, University of Toronto

Khaemba, W. 2018a. *Science Granting Councils Initiative in sub-Saharan Africa. Strengthening partnerships among Africa's Science granting councils and the private sector. A baseline assessment of public-private partnerships in research and scientific cooperation in Botswana.* African Centre for Technology Studies (ACTS). https://www.acts-net.org/images/SGCI/Baseline-Reports/Baseline-Report-Botswana.pdf

Khaemba, W. 2018b. *Science Granting Councils Initiative in sub-Saharan Africa. Strengthening partnerships among Africa's Science granting councils and the private sector. A baseline assessment of public-private partnerships in research and scientific cooperation in Kenya.* African Centre for Technology Studies (ACTS). https://www.acts-net.org/images/SGCI/Baseline-Reports/Baseline-Report-Kenya.pdf

Khaemba, W. 2018c. A Baseline Assessment of Public-Private Partnerships in Research and Scientific Cooperation in Botswana. *SGCI in Sub-Saharan Africa*

Kimenyi, M. S., Mwega, F. M. and Ndung'u, N. S. 2016. The African Lions: Kenya Country Case Study. In Bhorat, H. and Tarp, F. (Eds), *Africa's Lions: Growth Traps and Opportunities for Six African Economies.* Brookings Institution Press. https://www.wider.unu.edu/publication/kenya-0

Koehn, P. H. and Uitto, J. I. 2015. Beyond Outputs: Pathways to Symmetrical Evaluations of University Sustainable Development Partnerships. *Development Studies Research,* 2(1), 1–19. DOI: 10.1080/21665095.2015.1006732

Koenig, M. 2005. The Links Between Academic Research and Public Policy in the Field of Migration and Ethnic Relations: Selected National Case Studies. *International Journal of Multicultural Societies,* 7(1), 1–2

Konig, T. 2017. *The European Research Council.* Polity

Koyi, S., Kiprono, C. Z. and George, M. 2020. Higher Education Trajectory in Kenya: Historical Lessons and Prospects for Universities. *African Journal of Emerging Issues,* 2(13), 1–12

Kunda, D., Chembe, C. and Mukupa, G. 2018. Factors that Influence Zambian Higher Education Lecturer's attitude towards Integrating ICTs in Teaching and Research. *Journal of Technology and Science Education,* 8(4), 360–384

Larmer, M. 2006. What Went Wrong? Zambian Political Biography and Post-Colonial Discourses of Decline, *Historia,* 51(1), 235–256

Lefa, B. J. 2014. History of Higher Education in South Africa. *History and Background of South African Education* (July)

Lindgren, J. H., and Kehoe W. J. 1981. Focus Groups: Approaches, procedures and implications. *Learning Disabilities: Research and Practice,* 11, 96–106

Lugo-Gil, J., Jean-Baptiste, D. and Jaramilo, L. F. 2019. *Use of Evidence to Drive Decision-making in Government.* US Department of Health and Human Services

Macey, D. 2000. *The Penguin Dictionary of Critical Theory.* Penguin

Maobe, A. K. and Liping, P. 2020. Higher Education Reforms in Kenya: Options and Development. International Center for Teacher Education, East China Normal University (January)

Masaiti, G. & Mwale, N. 2020. The Drive and Nature of Internationalisation of Higher Education in Zambia. *International Journal of African Higher Education,* 7(2), 199–121

Mbiganyi, M. 2018. Factors Shaping Higher Education in Botswana: A Recipe for Policy Formulation and Implementation? *International Journal of Learning and Teaching,* 4(1), 64–69

Mbiganyi, M., Garegope, G., Mompei, S., Maokaneng, K., Isaac, P. and Mooketsi, U. 2015. Knowledge Society for Africa: Creating a Coherence Roadmap in the Science, Technology and Innovation (STI) Pillar in Botswana. https://www.researchgate.net/publication/320490276_Knowledge_society_for_Africa_Creating_a_Coherence_Roadmap_in_Science_Technology_and_Innovation_STI_pillar_in_Botswana

McCowan, T. 2018. Quality of Higher Education in Kenya: Addressing the Conundrum. *International Journal of Educational Development,* 60, 128–137

Ministry of Higher Education (MOHE). 2019. *Higher Education Policy 2019.* MOHE.

Ministry of Tertiary Education, Research, Science and Technology (MTERST). 2021. Research and Development. MTTRST. http://www.mttrst.gov.bw/research-and-development

Mohajan, H. K. 2013. Poverty and Economic Development of Kenya. *International Journal of Information Technology and Business Management,* 18(1), 72–82

Moja, T., and Cloete, N. (1996). Transforming Higher Education in South Africa: A New Approach to Governance. *Issue: A Journal of Opinion,* 24(1), 10–16

Molutsi, P. D. 2009. *Tertiary Education Reforms in Botswana.* Commonwealth Education Partnerships. https://www.cedol.org/wp-content/uploads/2012/02/136-138-2009.pdf

Mose, N. G. 2021. Determinants of Regional Economic Growth in Kenya. *African Journal of Business Management,* 15(1), 1–12. DOI: 10.5897/AJBM2020.9118

Moses, C., Sithole, M. M., Blankley, W., Labadarios, D., Makelane, H. and Nkobole, N. 2012. The State of Innovation in South Africa: Findings from the South African National Innovation Survey. *South African Journal of Science,* 108(7/8), 1–5. http://dx/doi.org/10.4102/sajs.v108i7/8.1320

Mouton, J. 2006. Science for Transformation: Research Agendas and Priorities in South Africa. In Box, L. and Engelhard, R. (Eds), *Science and Technology Policy for Development: Dialogues at the Interface.* Anthem

Mouton, J. 2008. The State of Social Science in Sub-Saharan Africa. In: *World Social Science Report* (63–67). UNESCO Publishing

Mouton, J., Basson, I., Blanckenberg, I., Boshoff, N., Prozesky, H., Redelinghuys, H., Treptow, R., Van Lill, M. and Van Niekerk, M. 2019. *The State of South Africa Research Enterprise.* DST-NRF Centre of Excellence in Scientrometics and Science, Technology and Policy, Stellenbosch University

Mouton, J. and Valentine, A. 2017. The Extent of South Africa Authored Articles in Predatory Journals. *South Africa Journal of Sciences,* 113(7/8), Art #2017-0010. http://dx.doi.org/10.17159/sajs.2017/20170010

Mouton, J., Gaillard, J. and Van Lill, M. 2015. Functions of Science Granting Councils in Sub-Saharan Africa. In Cloete, N., Maassen, P. and Bailey, T. (Eds), *Knowledge Production and Contradictory Functions in African Higher Education* (148-170). African Minds. https://doi.org/10.5281/zenodo.824879

Mouton, J., Gaillard, J. and Van Lill, M. 2014. *Science Granting Councils in Sub-Saharan Africa, Final Technical Report.* International Development Research Centre (IDRC)

Mukhwana, E. J., Too, J., Kande, A. and Nandokha, H. 2020. Financing Higher Education in Africa: The Case of Kenya. *African Journal of Rural Development,* 5(3), 53–64

Mukwena, M. 2021. The Internationalisation of Higher Education Institutes (HEIs) in the Southern Africa Development Community (SADC): A Comparative Content Analysis. *International Journal of Research and Innovation in Social Science,* 5(2), 216–222

Mulongo, G. 2013. Inequality in Accessing Higher Education in Kenya: Implications for Economic Development and Well-being. *International Journal of Humanities and Social Science,* 3(16), 49–61

Musiige, G. and Maasen, P. 2015. Faculty Perceptions of the Factors that Influence Research Productivity as Makerere University. In Cloete, N., Maassen, P. and Bailey, T. (Eds), *Knowledge Production and Contradictory Functions in African Higher Education* (109-127). African Minds. https://doi.org/10.5281/zenodo.824662

National Research Council. 2008. *Rebuilding the Research Capacity at HUD.* National Academic Press

National Research Foundation (NRF). 2019. *The NRF Industry Partnership Strategy.* https://www.nrf.ac.za/wp-content/uploads/2021/05/The-NRF-Industry-Partnership-Strategy.pdf

Naude, C. E., Zani, B., Ongolo-Zogo, P., Wiysonge, C. S., Dudley, L., Kredo, T., Garner, P. and Young, T. 2015. Research Evidence and Policy: Qualitative Study in Selected Provinces in South Africa and Cameroon. *Implementation Science,* 10(126), 1–10

Ndemwa, N. and Otani, M. 2020. Education System in Kenya: Its Current Condition and Challenges, *Minutes of the Faculty of Education, Shimane University (Education Science),* 53(2) 15–26

Ndunda, M. and Maina, F. (2021). Creating an environment for intellectual capital remittance. *University World News Africa Edition* (16 December). https://www.universityworldnews.com/post.php?story=20211101095524471

Nkwe, N. 2012. E-Government: Challenges and Opportunities in Botswana, *International Journal of Humanities and Social Science,* 2(17), 39-48

Nutley, S., Davies, H. and Walter, I. 2002. Evidence-Based Policy and Practice: Cross Sector Lessons from the UK. *Working Paper* No. 9. ESRC UK Centre for Evidence-Based Policy and Practice

Nyadera, I. N., Agwanda, B. and Maulani, N. 2020. Evolution of Kenya's Political System and Challenges to Democracy. In Farazmand, A. (Ed.), *Global Encyclopedia of Public Administration, Public Policy and Governance.* Springer Nature

Odhiambo, G. 2018. The Role of Kenyan Universities in National Development. *FIRE: Forum for International Research in Education,* 4(3), 191–209

Ogada, T., Sange, S. and Mboya, R. 2015. *Establishing Robust Institutional IP Policies and Strategies for Sustainable Public Private Partnership: Case of Kenya.* Science Technology and Innovation for the Transformation of African Economies

Olomola, A. S. 2007. An Analysis of the Research–Policy Nexus in Nigeria. In Ayuk, E. T. and Maouani, M. A. (Eds), *The Policy Paradox in Africa: Strengthening Links between Economic Research and Policymaking* (165–184). Africa World Press

Ooro, S. 2009. *The Quest for Inclusive Higher Education in Kenya: A Vivisection of Concerns, Policies and Reform Initiatives.* OCIDES Publications

Osagie, R. O. 2012. Federal Government Funding of Research in Universities in Nigeria: The University of Benin as a Case Study. *International Education Studies,* 5(6), 73–79

Oyelaran-Oyeyinka, B., Vallejo, B., Abejirin, B., Vusudev, S., Ozor, N. and Bolo, M. 2018. Towards Effective Public–Private Partnerships in Research and Innovation: A Perspective for African Science Granting Councils, *ATPS Technopolicy Brief* No. 49

Oyeniran, R. 2017. Basic Education in Ivory Coast: From Education for All to Compulsory Education, Challenges and Perspectives. *Journal of Education and Learning,* 6(2), 283–293

Oyeniran, R. 2018. Education for All in Developing Countries: A Critical Analysis of Ivorian Educational System. *Journal of Educational System,* 2(2), 25–33

Ozor, N., Bolo, M., Oriama, R. and Musila, F. 2020. *Networking Africa's Science Granting Councils: Building partnerships and networks among science granting councils and other science system actors in sub-Saharan Africa. ATPS Final Technical Report.* IDRC. https://idl-bnc-idrc.dspacedirect.org/bitstream/handle/10625/58621/58758.pdf

Public Servants' Association (PSA). 2016. Fixing Higher Education in South Africa: A PSA Perspective. *PSA Choice* (July)

Raphasha, P. I. 2015. *Integrating National and Regional Innovation Policy: The Case of Gauteng in South Africa.* Master's thesis submitted to the Wits Business School, University of Witwatersand

Rawls, J. 1971. *A Theory of Justice.* Belknap Press

Rawls, J. 2001. *Justice as Fairness: A Restatement.* Belknap Press

Republic of Botswana. 2022. Ministry of Tertiary Education, Research, Science and Technology. Web page. http://www.gov.bw/ministries/ministry-tertiary-education-research-science-and-technology

Republic of Kenya Ministry of Science and Technology. 2008. *Science Technology and Innovation Policy and Strategy,* Nairobi, March

Republic of Kenya. 2012. A Policy Framework for Science, Technology and Innovation: Revitalizing and Harnessing Science Technology and Innovation in Kenya, *Ministry of Higher Education Science Technology Sessional Paper* No. 2012

Republic of Kenya. 2014. *Laws of Kenya: Science Technology and Innovation Act No. 28 of 2013 (revised edition 2014).* National Council for Law Reporting

Republic of Kenya. 2015. *Sector Plan for Science Technology and Innovation 2013–2017; Revitalising and Harnessing Science, Technology and Innovation for Kenya's Prosperity and Global Competitiveness.* Republic of Kenya

Republic of South Africa. 2019. *White Paper on Science, Technology and Innovation.* Department of Science and Technology

Republic of Zambia. 1996. *National Policy on Science and Technology, May 1996.* Ministry of Science, Technology and Vocational Training

Republic of Zambia. 2017. *Report of the Committee on Education, Science and Technology for the First Session of the Twelfth National Assembly appointed on Thursday 6 October 2016.* National Assembly of Zambia

Republic of Zambia. 2017. *Seventh National Development Plan 2017–2021.* Ministry of National Development Planning

Rugut, M. 2014. Science, Technology and Innovation for Sustainable Development. 3rd Annual Biosafety Conference, KICC Nairobi, 11–14 August

Samboma, T. A. 2019. E-Government: A Tool for Service Delivery in Botswana's Local Authorities? *Global Journal of Human-Social Science: F Political Science,* 19(1), 1-6

Science Granting Councils Initiative (SGCI). 2017. *Towards Effective Public-Private Partnerships in Research and Innovation: Research Grant Concept Note and Terms of Reference.* SGCI

Science Granting Councils Initiative (SGCI). 2018a. *New Approaches for Funding Research and Innovation in Africa.* SGCI

Science Granting Councils Initiative (SGCI). 2018b. *Commissioned Studies: Public–Private Partnerships in Research and Innovation.* SGCI

Science Granting Councils Initiative (SGCI). 2019. Open Science in Research and Innovation for Development. SGCI

Science Granting Councils Initiative (SGCI). 2021. *Public Engagement in Research and Innovation for Development.* SGCI

Sebola, M. P. 2023. South Africa's Public Higher Education Institutions, University Research Outputs, and Contribution to National Human Capital. *Human Resource Development International,* 26(2), 217–231

Sen, A. 2009. *The Idea of Justice.* Belknap Press

Sheikheldin, G. 2018. *Science Granting Councils Initiative (SGCI) in Sub-Saharan Africa: Strengthening Partnerships among Africa's Science Granting Councils and the Private Sector. A Baseline Assessment of Public–Private Partnerships in Research and Scientific Cooperation in Zambia.* Science, Technology and Innovation Policy Research Organization (STIPRO). https://www.acts-net.org/images/SGCI/Baseline-Reports/Baseline-Report-Zambia.pdf

Soare, L. 2013. Creating a Linkage between Academic Research and Policy-making. *Europolity*, 7(2), 89–102.

Space in Africa. 2020. South Africa Cuts Science and Innovation Budget: Announces Plan for the Future. 27 July. https://africanews.space/south-africa-cuts-science-and-innovation-budget-announces-plan-for-the-future/

Ssebuwufu, J., Ludwick, T. and Beland, M. 2012. Strengthening University-Industry Linkages in Africa: A Study on Institutional Capacities and Gaps. Accra: Association of African Universities

Statistics Botswana. 2022. Botswana Data At-a-Glance. https://botswana.opendataforafrica.org/

St John E. P. 2013. Tools of State: Using Research to Inform Policy Decisions in Higher Education. *International and Multidisciplinary Journal of Social Sciences,* 2(2), 118-144. DOI:10.4471/rimcis.2013.17

Tamilenthi, S. and Junior, L. E. (2011). The Barriers of Higher Education in the African Countries of Zambia and Tanzania. *Archives of Applied Science Research,* 3(4),169–178

Teng-Zeng, F. 2009. *Mapping Research Systems in Developing Countries, Country Report: The Science and Technology System of Botswana.* UNESCO, CREST and IRD

Teseletso, T. 2021. BIUST's Physics & Astronomy Department Hosts DARA Training. *BIUST News* (20 September). https://www.biust.ac.bw/blog/biusts-physics-astronomy-department-hosts-dara-training/

Tigabu, A. and Khaemba, W. 2020. Science Granting Councils in Africa: Catalysts of Innovation for Sustainable Development. *Public Policy*, 32(3), 199–209

Tijssen, R. and Kraemer-Mbula, E. 2018. Research Excellence in Africa: Policies, Perceptions, and Performance. *Science and Public Policy*, 45(3), 392–403

Tumuti, D. W., Wanderi, P. M., & Lang'at-Thoruwa, C. 2013. Benefits of University–Industry Partnerships: The Case of Kenyatta University and Equity Bank. *International Journal of Business and Social Science*, 4(7), 26–33

United Nations Conference on Trade and Development (UNCTAD). 2017. *The Missing Link between Growth and Development: The Case of Copper-dependent Zambia. Background Document to the Commodities and Development Report 2017.* UNCTAD

United Nations Conference on Trade and Development (UNCTAD). 2021. *Economic Development in Africa Report 2021: Reaping the Potential Benefits of the African Continental Free Trade Area for Inclusive Growth.* United Nations

United Nations Conference on Trade and Development (UNCTAD). 2022. *Science, Technology and Innovation Policy Review of Zambia.* United Nations

United Nations Development Programme (UNDP). 2010. *Assessment of Development Results Zambia: Evaluation of UNDP Contribution.* UNDP

United Nations Development Programme (UNDP). 2014. *The Impacts of Social and Economic Inequality on Economic Development in South Africa.* UNDP

United Nations Development Programme (UNDP). 2021. Botswana. UNDP. https://www.bw.undp.org/

United Nations Economic Commissions for Africa (UNECA). 2014. *National Experiences in the Transfer of Publicly Funded Technologies in Africa: Ghana, Kenya and Zambia.* UNECA

United Nations Economic Commission for Africa (UNECA). 2017. *Country Profile 2016 – South Africa.* UNECA

United Nations South Africa (UNSA). 2020. *Common Country Analysis.* UNSA

Universalia. 2018. *Summative Evaluation of GPE's Country-Level Support to Education, Batch 2, Country 3: Cote d'Ivoire.* Universalia Final Report (V3), August

University World News. 2021. Creating vibrant and stronger research communities. *University World News Africa Edition* (16 December). https://www.universityworldnews.com/post.php?story=20211215131016702

Van Lill, M. and Gaillard, J. 2014. *Science Granting Councils in Sub-Saharan Africa – Country Report: Cote d'Ivoire.* CREST and IRD

Van Schalkwyk, F. 2015. University Engagement as Interconnectedness: Indicators and Insights. In Cloete, N., Maassen, P. and Bailey, T. (Eds), *Knowledge Production and Contradictory Functions in African Higher Education* (203–229). African Minds. https://doi.org/10.5281/zenodo.824885

Wairegi, S. G. W. 2021. Role of Science and Technology in Advancing National Security in 21st Century Africa: A Case Study of Kenya. Master's thesis submitted to the Institute of Diplomacy and International Studies, University of Nairobi

Waruru, M. 2021. Researchers Failing 'Relevance Test', Some HE Ministers Say. *University World News Africa Edition* (10 December). https://www.universityworldnews.com/post.php?story=20211210065625160

Weaver, A., Pefile, S., Walwyn, D., Eksteen, J., Chiepe, G. and Maphanyane, E. 2005. *Botswana National Research, Science and Technology Plan – Final Report.* CSIR

World Bank. 2019a. *Improving Higher Education Performance in Kenya: A Policy Report.* The World Bank.

World Bank. 2019b. International Development Association Project Appraisal Document on a Proposed Credit in the Amount of EUR 88 million to the Republic of Côte d'Ivoire for the Côte d'Ivoire Higher Education Development Support Project (1 March). The World Bank

World Bank. 2021. *Feasibility Study to Connect all African Higher Education Institutions to High-Speed Internet: Côte d'Ivoire Case Study.* The World Bank

About the Authors

PROF. TEBOHO MOJA is a Professor of Higher Education at New York University, an Extraordinary Professor at the University of the Western Cape (South Africa), and a Visiting Research Fellow at the Centre for the Advancement of Scholarship at the University of Pretoria (South Africa). She was awarded an Honorary Doctorate in 2021 by the University of Pretoria. She is the recipient of the Martin Luther King jr Faculty Award (2019), the National Research Foundation Lifetime Achiever Award (2019), Women in International Education Award (2019), and the Graduate Students Star Award (2019). She has published widely in the area of higher education and delivered numerous keynote addresses. She is the Editor-in-Chief for the *Journal of Student Affairs in Africa* and serves on several other editorial boards. She has also held visiting professorship in several international universities.

DR SAMUEL KEHINDE OKUNADE holds a doctorate degree in Conflict Transformation and Peace Studies from the University of KwaZulu-Natal (South Africa). He researches on borders and youth out-migration, most especially as it concerns human trafficking and migrant smuggling in Africa. As an early career researcher in Africa confronted with several challenges which many early career researchers face on the continent, his attention has been drawn toward delving into these issues empirically and proffering solutions. His fields of interest cut across borderland studies, security studies, peace and conflict studies, development studies, migration, refugee studies, and higher education studies.